Low Tech Life

—·—

A Guide to Mindful Digital Minimalism

Jose Briones

Copyright © 2023 by Jose Briones

All rights reserved.

No portion of this book may be reproduced in any form without written permission from the publisher or author, except as permitted by U.S. copyright law.

Contents

Prologue	VI
1. Gaining weight and spending money	1
Getting into Debt	
2. Should I get a dumbphone?	11
Living without convenience	
Directions	
Music	
Communication Apps	
So, should I purchase a dumbphone?	
3. I want a dumbphone, but which one?	33
Carrier Compatibility	
Operating Systems	
What makes a dumbphone a dumbphone?	
Recommendations	
4. I don't want a dumbphone, but my screentime is awful!	53
Size Matters	

Design Matters
   Reduce, Replace, Reframe.
   Recommendations

5. Mastering Boredom   72
   Pick up the pace
   Calming Your Mind
   Creating Community
   Embracing Boredom

6. What will my family think?   93
   Who are you doing this for?
   Make the most when you are present
   Keep yourself (and your family) sane
   The Foyer and the Ethernet Room

7. Is my profession compatible with low tech?   105
   VBLCCP
   Second Factor Authentication
   Mindful Mail
   Working Online

8. Being a good example   121
   From Software to Satiety
   Handling a small business with balance
   Screentime for family's sake
   Peer to Peer Leadership
   Setting up the best example

9. My Low Tech Lifestyle — 135
   E-Ink vs LCD
   Operating Systems: Ya Basic
   Television: A Conscious Decision to Disconnect
   Embracing Gaming, but Limiting it to the Office
   A Day in My Life: Balancing Work, Play, and Mindfulness

10. Creating a low tech lifestyle — 148
    Step 1: Make an Inventory and Categorize
    Step 2: Quit Services
    Step 3: Time Zones
    Step 4: Companions (another name for accountability and helpful tools)
    Step 5: Repeat

11. Conclusion — 164

Epilogue — 166

Prologue

I am deeply grateful that you've chosen to embark on this journey towards mindful digital minimalism with me. Opening the cover of this book is the first step, and I want to express my heartfelt appreciation for your courage to explore a path less taken, one that dares to challenge our society's norm of hyperconnectivity. 'Low Tech Life: A Guide to Mindful Digital Minimalism' is a tapestry of stories, insights, and practical tips, all carefully curated to assist you in reducing your digital consumption. This book is not a one-size-fits-all blueprint, but rather a guide that acknowledges the deeply personal nature of our relationship with technology. It's my hope that within these pages, you'll find the inspiration and guidance needed to carve out your unique path towards a more mindful, fulfilling digital life.

Throughout this book, you will encounter a myriad of stories, some recounting personal experiences, others borrowed from individuals who've successfully navigated their way towards digital minimalism. These narratives serve as a testament to the possibility of a healthier, more balanced relationship with technology. Coupled with these stories, you will find practical strategies and step-by-step guides designed to help you declutter your digital life. These tools are intended to empower you, providing the means to evaluate, manage, and, where necessary, reduce your digital consumption. They are the culmination of years of exploration and experimentation in the realm of digital minimalism.

However, this book is not a magic wand that will instantly transform your digital habits. Instead, it is a compass – a tool to guide you in the right direction. Remember, this journey towards a low-tech life is a personal one. It will take time, and there will be challenges along the way. There might be moments of self-doubt, and perhaps even setbacks, but do not be discouraged. Each stumble is a learning opportunity, each obstacle, a call for resilience. One of the central tenets of this book is that digital minimalism isn't about renouncing technology; it's about using it in a way that serves you, instead of allowing it to become your master. It's about recognizing the value of your attention and investing it in ways that truly enrich your life.

As you delve into the following pages, I invite you to keep an open mind, to be patient with yourself, and, above all, to relish this journey towards a low tech life. My sincerest wish is that this book will guide you, enlighten you, and, most importantly, inspire you to take control of your digital life.

Thank you for beginning this journey. Now, let's step forward together into the mindful world of digital minimalism.

Warmly,

Jose Briones

Chapter 1

Gaining Weight and Spending Money

As I gazed at my reflection in the mirror, I was struck by a stark realization - I had gained 20 pounds since earning my Master's degree just a year prior. Once an avid gym-goer, I now found myself sedentary, frequently indulging in fast food like pizza and Funyuns while binge-watching Netflix. This transformation wasn't due to any deliberate choice, physical injury, dietary change, or depression. My lifestyle had simply shifted, and I had failed to keep pace with my body's evolving needs. Convenience had taken precedence over intention, and I found myself reaching for more Papa Johns pizzas than I'd like to admit. My attention had shifted from self-care to career advancement, causing me to overlook the gradual changes that were occurring in my day-to-day life. But I don't fault myself, for this is often how life unfolds - it races by, and changes materialize subtly. My once active routine of morning runs, attending classes, and socializing with friends had been replaced with long office hours, returning home exhausted, and seeking comfort in entertainment.

Though this book's primary focus is not on weight management, the story above underscores the importance of acknowledging the ever-changing nature of our lives and the need for continuous adjustment. Confronted with my dissatisfaction regarding my weight gain, I resolved to take action by adopting a detox program that aimed to reduce my caloric intake. This 30-day regimen involved consuming granola for breakfast, salads for lunch, and fruit for dinner. Despite the accolades this program received from many of its adherents, my initial attempt was unsuccessful. This experience served to emphasize a key point that will be reiterated throughout the book: detoxes, while they may appear advantageous, are not viable long-term solutions. Instead of fixating on deprivation, we must prioritize reconfiguring our habits to achieve lasting change. This approach resembles adopting a marathoner's mindset rather than relying on short bursts of effort to attain our objectives. Throughout the following pages, I'll aim to guide you in developing the attitudes and practices through stories and research for achieving sustainable success in various digital aspects of life.

My failed attempt at a detox in 2019 had nothing to do with salads being less tasty or nutritious than other foods. It was due to the fact that I tried to reintroduce salads to my diet while ignoring the reality that my body had grown accustomed to consuming margherita pizzas from Panera and garlic sauce pineapple pizzas from Papa Johns. Although I wanted to remove the junk food out of my life, my automatic behavior said otherwise. I craved the cheesy and greasy pizzas, and my body was used to the taste and texture. It was difficult to make the switch to salads without feeling deprived and unsatisfied. As Wendy Wood notes in her article Habit Formation and Change, "habits are stored in procedural memory relatively separate from goals and intentions, encountering the same context activates habitual responses, even when newly adopted intentions are strong."[1] Despite my best intentions, I found myself reverting to my old habits because my environment and context remained the same.

Furthermore, research conducted by Benjamin Gardner and his colleagues demonstrates that gradually integrating new habits into our lives and modifying our environment are more effective methods for maintaining resolutions. Gardner contends that "forming a habit is about discovering ways to make actions 'unthinking' and automatic so that they seamlessly blend into the context in which they occur."[2] With this in mind, instead of attempting to abruptly eliminate pizza from my diet and replace it with salads, I could have slowly introduced greens into my meals while gradually reducing my intake of fast food. Including vegetables and other nutritious items alongside my current eating habits would have fostered positive associations in my brain, rather than fixating on the bland sensation left by lettuce and carrots in my palate. Unfortunately, my detox attempt lasted a mere three days before I succumbed to the temptation of my former eating habits. Feeling guilty about my lack of discipline, I called the nearby pizzeria and indulged in an extra-large pizza for dinner.

As Wendy Wood underscores, "New directions in habit change encompass not only altering beliefs and perceptions but also utilizing cognitive strategies (e.g., reminders) in conjunction with environmental change strategies." It is, therefore, essential to recognize that willpower alone is insufficient to break a bad habit; we must also create a conducive environment, adopt new habits incrementally, and allow for substitutions to achieve success. In 2022, I began to introduce greens more intentionally into my diet. By positioning them next to appealing dishes and consuming them first thing in the morning, I fostered an environment that enabled me to indulge while prioritizing greens and plant-based foods. This approach helped strike a balance between enjoying treats and maintaining a nutritious diet. For instance, I now savor an egg or two atop cherry tomatoes and spinach leaves, making the habit change more sustainable in the long run. Additionally, incorporating visual cues, such as displaying fruits and vegetables prominently or seeking out recipes rich in plant-based ingredients, has further reinforced my commitment to healthier eating habits. After all my sorrows, I've come to the realization that eating healthy is a choice. One that must be learned and prioritized.

Getting into Debt

There was a pivotal moment in my personal journey that I'll never forget: the day I opened a balance transfer card. Back in 2016, during my graduate school years, I obtained my first credit card from Discover. The card came with a manageable limit of $500 and generous cashback rewards. Despite not having a substantial salary, I managed to double the credit card company's given amount by treating it like a debit card and paying the balance in full every day. This strategy worked well for a while, and I felt confident in my ability to manage my finances. By paying my credit card like a debit, I thought I could avoid any interest charges and continue to create space in my budget for little luxuries here and there. However, like many Americans, I did not have a plan for my budget in place. Discover, on the other hand, did.

Sachin Banker and his colleagues conducted a study that indicates credit card usage can have an impact on spending habits, potentially leading to increased overall spending. According to their research, individuals who use credit cards are more likely to spend more money than those who use cash or debit cards. The study's findings showed that "participants were more willing to purchase higher-price items with credit rather than with cash, and thus they spent more overall when using [a] credit card (average basket = $87.41) rather than cash ($84.19)."[3] Furthermore, it revealed that "the neural signature associated with credit purchases is not price-contingent, and is instead reflected by differential activation in reward-related [regions of the brain], regardless of the price." As scary as their findings are, the research suggests that having a credit card affects our brains neurologically and invites us to spend more without considering the consequences. Additionally, the study found that credit cards might reduce our sensitivity to the prices of the products we buy. The authors noted, "credit cards reduce sensitivity to price information via heightened striatal activation, exhibited during the periods in which product price is presented to participants." This decreased sensitivity to prices can make it easier for individuals to justify purchasing more expensive items or indulging in unnecessary luxuries—something that I, myself, am all too familiar with.

In June 2018, life threw a curveball at me in the form of a medical emergency, causing all my carefully laid plans to unravel. By this point, my credit limit had ballooned from $500 to $5,000, and although I was still making daily payments, my student status meant that my income hadn't grown enough to create an adequately funded emergency fund. Financial experts typically recommend having at least $1,500 set aside for emergencies, but I only had a meager $300 in savings. Looking back, I now realize that my spending habits were influenced by my credit card usage, which led me to make erratic and impulsive purchases. I often gave in to the temptation of the local baguette shop, Baguette De France, and skipped grocery runs, which could have helped me save money. I convinced myself that I would make more money after graduation and could pay off my debts as I exited Best Buy with the latest generation Surface Laptop. My brain had become accustomed to swiping without thinking about the consequences, and my credit card usage had automatized my purchases, making it easier to justify these luxuries. At that time, I didn't realize that having a credit card could affect my spending behavior and lead me to accumulate more debt than I could handle.

Despite thinking that I had it all figured out with my new credit limit and daily payments, that 2018 visit to the hospital changed my financial trajectory for the next five years. I chose to pay $1,500 through credit instead of a payment plan, thinking I could handle it with a recent raise and collect some cashback along the way. Little did I know that this seemingly innocuous decision would spiral into a massive $5,000 debt. Discover's marketing had worked on me. I fell into the same trap as my parents, living beyond my means and rationalizing my purchases with rewards points. In hindsight, I realized that financial security requires a complete shift in mindset and habits, and the path to recovery would be long and arduous. In my desperate attempt to resolve my mounting debt, I stumbled upon an enticing "solution" that seemed to offer relief: a balance transfer card. It appeared to be a quick fix, a way to simply move my debt from one credit card to another while lowering my interest rate to zero. I convinced myself that I had found a solution, that I was being proactive. But the reality was that I had merely transferred my problems from Discover to Chase, opening up a new $6,000 credit line for myself and indulging in even more unnecessary luxuries.

The cycle continued. I didn't have a plan, yet Discover and Chase did. My debt ballooned to an astonishing $10,000. It was only then that I realized the hard truth: transferring our problems is not the answer. In this book, I will share with you the importance of finding sustainable solutions that address the root causes of our digital struggles, rather than just shifting the burden elsewhere. By adopting this mindset, we can pave the way for a brighter and more sustainable approach to technology. Facing a mountain of debt and financial uncertainty, I knew I had to make a change. With a staggering $35,000 in student loans and consumer debt, I was at a loss for how to begin. Through careful research of financial books and personal reflection, I was able to finally have what all the big banks had: a plan. Together, my fiancee and I created a 18-month spending plan to reduce my burden and take back control of my finances. No longer would I waste money on frivolous purchases like high-tech gadgets or dining out at expensive restaurants. Instead, I was to focus on reducing my expenses and sticking to the family budget. I switched my postpaid cellphone plan from T-mobile to a prepaid one through US Mobile. I bought a car vacuum and a bucket to clean the car instead of using the carwash. She even prompted me to sell some of my furniture instead of enjoying the nice decor collection I had built. It wasn't easy, but after four years of intense dedication, I emerged from my financial struggles stronger and more secure than ever before.

As we navigate the complexities of our technologically-driven world, it's more important than ever to be mindful of our digital dependencies. By understanding the landscape of our technological habits and devising a plan to minimize our use, we can regain control over our time and attention. With the right tools and techniques at our disposal, we can learn to navigate our digital lives with intention and purpose. Thus, join me as we explore the world of digital minimalism and tackle one of the most common questions facing those looking to reduce their tech use: is a dumbphone right for you?

1. Carden, L., & Wood, W. (2018). Habit formation and change. Current Opinion in Behavioral Sciences, 20, 117-122. https://doi.org/10.1016/j.cobeha.2017.12.014
2. Gardner, B., Rebar, A. L., & Lally, P. (2022). How does habit form? Guidelines for tracking real-world habit formation. Cogent Psychology, 9(1), Article 2041277. https://doi.org/10.1080/23311908.2022.2041277
3. Banker, S., Dunfield, D., Huang, A., & Prelec, D. (2021). Neural mechanisms of credit card spending. Scientific Reports, 11(1), Article 4070. https://doi.org/10.1038/s41598-021-83488-3

Chapter 2

Should I get a dumbphone?

The winter of 2019 was frigid and dreary, yet I resolved to take charge of my digital life. Overwhelmed by my smartphone, I decided it was time to switch things up. Embracing this newfound determination, I replaced my smartphone with the Light Phone 2, a minimalist device offering only essential features. This refreshing transition aimed to liberate me from my reliance on digital devices. Initially, adapting to the basic phone's constraints proved challenging. The absence of social media and other familiar apps left me feeling disconnected from my social circle. I longed for the convenience of browsing my newsfeed or accessing my email on the move. Nonetheless, I reminded myself that this transformation was for the better and resolved to persevere.

In the beginning, I naively assumed that a simpler phone would cure my digital addiction. However, as the weeks passed and external conditions remained uncertain, I experienced a startling revelation: the issue was not the device itself but my insatiable desire for constant information. After a decade of smartphone use, my brain had become wired for convenience. The iPhone had merely facilitated my unhealthy habits. The device, itself, was not the root cause. Clicking through the browser, finding directions to restaurants, and refreshing email were second nature to me. At the core was my innate desire to stay perpetually connected to the online world, a need intensified by the pandemic's unprecedented circumstances. With the iPhone gone, I merely found another outlet for this obsession, my laptop. My choice of device had shifted, but the underlying habit tenaciously persisted. I recognized that escaping my digital dependence necessitated more than a mere hardware change; it demanded a mindset transformation and a deeper comprehension of my motivations. Only then could I genuinely embark on the journey towards a more balanced and mindful relationship with technology.

Unexpectedly, a global pandemic soon struck, bringing life as we knew it to a standstill. While my new phone's limitations curbed my screen time outdoors, I found myself retreating indoors more frequently. Craving connection to the outside world, I turned to my laptop for solace. Consequently, I spent hours surfing the web, watching shows, and immersing myself in video games. As the weeks went by, FIFA 20 became my go-to source of entertainment. Offering a much-needed reprieve from the unsettling reality outside, I lost myself in its virtual world for hours. Regrettably, my overall screen time increased rather than diminished after changing to a simpler phone. This realization served as a humbling reminder that I needed to monitor my digital habits, even during the most difficult periods.

In hindsight, my experience with the Light Phone 2 and the pandemic imparted a crucial lesson. It is easy to succumb to the convenience and appeal of digital devices, but being aware of their impact on our lives is vital. While we cannot always control external circumstances, we can manage our interactions with technology. By practicing mindfulness and intentionality in our digital habits, we can foster a healthier and more balanced relationship with technology.

In 2021, a study by Cristina Ghita and Claes Thorén highlighted the challenges individuals face when attempting to quit smartphones "cold turkey" by switching to dumbphones. In their autoethnographic research, they observed, "Our experiences indeed indicate that replacing the smartphone with a dumbphone increases producti vity... However, the dumbphone's simplicity introduces struggles, which we both perceived as significant enough to negatively affect us, leading to feelings of anxiety, frustration, and workarounds."[1] Their findings resonate with my 2020 experiment and the experiences shared within the dumbphone subreddit, a flourishing community of individuals who have deliberately chosen to defy the trend of smartphone usage. For those unfamiliar with Reddit, it is a social media platform that encourages discussions, questions, and the sharing of personal experiences among its users, who can opt to remain anonymous or use a pseudonym. A prevalent topic of conversation in the dumbphones subreddit centers on whether to transition to a basic cell phone to curb internet addiction. While the notion of adopting a dumbphone might appear to be an uncomplicated solution to reduce screen time, it may not prove to be a sustainable option for everyone within the subreddit community.

Similar to how transferring debt between credit cards may not address underlying financial issues, switching from a smartphone to a basic phone might not effectively tackle the root cause of excessive screen time. In fact, individuals often compensate for the absence of a smartphone by increasing their use of other devices, such as laptops, tablets, or smart TVs. A study published in the Journal of Computer-Mediated Communication revealed that participants experienced activation of the aversive motivational system, diminished cognitive performance, and heightened physiological anxiety levels when unable to answer their ringing iPhone.[2] Furthermore, the study sheds light on the theory that smart devices serve as an extension of ourselves due to the information we entrust to them. As we increasingly rely on our phones for storing and organizing various aspects of our lives, we form a deep connection with these devices. By assigning tasks like remembering phone numbers, storing notes, setting reminders, and managing other personal information to our phones, we inadvertently create a digital representation of our lives.

When our smartphones are taken away or replaced with more basic devices, we may feel disconnected and disoriented, as if a part of ourselves has been removed. This sense of disconnection stems from the loss of easy access to the wealth of sensitive information, personalized settings, and customized features that we've become accustomed to having at our fingertips. Consequently, our reliance on smartphones can lead to increased anxiety and decreased cognitive performance, as noted in the study above.[3]

While the glowing screen in our pockets may indeed be problematic, as we will discuss in Chapter 4, addressing excessive screen time requires more comprehensive strategies that focus not only on reducing smartphone usage but also on understanding and mitigating the factors that drive our dependence on these devices. Developing healthier habits, setting boundaries for screen time, and fostering greater self-awareness and self-regulation in our interactions with technology are essential. Merely changing the medium of consumption by streaming on a computer instead of a phone does not rewire the brain to adopt healthier digital habits. Additionally, individuals with addictive personalities may rationalize their usage of their preferred devices and postpone making meaningful changes. As I sustained continuous screen usage during the pandemic, I kept telling myself that it was a needed break for the stress coming from unprecedented circumstances. This behavior is comparable to delaying household chores and subsequently apologizing for not completing them on time. Many of us have experienced this common pattern with both chores and digital habits. We tend to justify our use of phones, laptops, or other devices by convincing ourselves that they are necessary for work. We may create the illusion of quickly checking something, when in reality, we are mindlessly scrolling through social media or getting lost in the internet's depths. For habits to stick, we must make deliberate decisions and allocate time for them, a routine request the soap in your counter makes for the unwashed plates inside the sink.

Living without convenience

As Thanksgiving 2015 approached, I eagerly anticipated my visit to my mother's home and spending time with her. Her home was always filled with warmth and love, and her cooking was something to behold. Unfortunately, a few days before the holiday, my mother's dishwasher stopped working. Despite calling a repairman, it became clear that it wouldn't be fixed in time for Thanksgiving dinner. Undaunted, my mother decided that we would wash the dishes by hand after the feast. With an old bottle of dish soap and a stack of sponges, we set to work. As we washed each dish, I felt a sense of nostalgia for the days when we didn't have a dishwasher and washing dishes by hand was a daily ritual in Nicaragua. There was a certain satisfaction that came from feeling the grime and grease give way beneath my fingers. As we worked together, chatting and laughing, I felt grateful for the opportunity to spend time with my mother and help her with the dishes. And as we scrubbed away, I realized that I had taken the convenience of a dishwasher for granted. In doing things the old-fashioned way, I gained a newfound appreciation for the simple pleasures of manual dishwashing.

The comparison of dishwashers to smartphones is fitting due to the convenience they both offer. Dishwashers and smartphones save time and provide services, albeit at different costs. The cost of a dishwasher is primarily monetary, while the cost of a smartphone can be more profound, impacting our minds, wallets, and personal relationships. Although dishwashers have advanced in recent years, they still cannot clean a recently finished casserole dish, just as smartphones cannot replace the benefits of face-to-face communication, deep thinking, and quality time spent with loved ones. Smartphones offer a level of convenience that can create an illusion of productivity and digital fulfillment, but it comes at a high cost to our overall well-being. In our pursuit of global connectedness through the internet, we may inadvertently neglect our closest relationships in favor of engaging with seemingly more "interesting" people online. While technology can be helpful to connect vulnerable people in our society[4], direct human relationships are still required to make those interactions meaningful. Among older adults, for example, using technology as a medium to reach family members and offer social support has had higher wellbeing impact than in younger members of society. As researchers have indagated, social isolation and smartphone addiction are positively related among younger populations. Their conclusions show that smart devices possess a certain power over our attention and time, which decreases our positive experiences in life.[5]

The pervasive presence of smart devices has contributed to a growing reliance on technology, as people increasingly embrace its advantages without fully considering the drawbacks. However, there is still hope. By counteracting the hurriedness often imposed by modern technologies, we can significantly improve our daily lives. In his book "The Ruthless Elimination of Hurry," John Mark Comer notes, "the solution to an overbusy life is not more time. It's to slow down and simplify our lives around what really matters."[6]Having adopted a slower lifestyle, Comer explains that doing less may result in fewer accolades in a society that values busyness, but it will also yield greater inner peace. This comes from eliminating excess and embracing a more purposeful way of living, which might involve tasks like "scrubbing casserole dishes by hand." Such a shift necessitates thoughtful planning and consideration, but the rewards are substantial: deeper connections with loved ones, heightened mindfulness, and a more intentional approach to everyday life. After using the Light Phone 2 for three years, I have come to understand that we often give up more than we realize in pursuit of convenience. As we become increasingly dependent on smart devices, we risk losing touch with how to live without the limitless wellspring of information available in our pockets.

Directions

One of the most pressing examples is directions. As we grow increasingly reliant on Google Maps, Apple Maps, and other digital navigation tools, we forget that there was a time when physical maps or asking people for directions was the main method of finding a place. This traditional method of navigation offered benefits that go beyond just getting from point A to point B. It allowed for a deeper and more meaningful engagement with our environment. Research on the usage of digital mapping for directions has shown that people who use GPS units or online maps reduce their sense of direction and spatial awareness significantly.[7] Moreover, other studies have illustrated that participants that used digital tools lost a sense of origin and length of the trip the more they used them.[8] By exploring unknown places without a voice guiding our every step, on the other hand, our hippocampus grows stronger. Moreover, relying on traditional methods of navigation also presented opportunities for external interaction with the world. Asking locals for directions not only allows us to find our way but also fosters a sense of community and trust.

During a trip to San Diego in February 2023, I decided to challenge myself by traveling without my trusty smart devices (iPad or Laptop). As a seasoned traveler, my previous default would have been to rely on an Uber or Lyft to get around town, or rent a car with GPS included. However, this time, I was determined to take a more old-school approach to getting around the city. Upon arriving at the airport, I made my way to the information desk and asked the attendant for recommendations on how to travel through the city. To my delight, the lady working that day was incredibly resourceful and knowledgeable about the area. She showed me how to get to downtown and which routes were best for walking or taking public transportation. I felt a sense of relief knowing that I didn't have to rely on vague internet advice or spend a fortune on ride-hailing services. Instead, I was able to trust the recommendations of a local and even learned how to use the Pronto card system for trolleys and buses. It was a refreshing change of pace and reminded me that sometimes, the most valuable information can be found by simply asking the right person.

These brief and shallow interactions with strangers could even lead to deeper connections and a sense of belonging in a new place. While digital navigation tools undoubtedly offer a level of convenience and ease, we must not forget the value of traditional methods of navigation. By relying too heavily on our smart devices, we risk losing the opportunity for meaningful engagement with our environment and the development of our own internal maps of the world. While the longterm effects of smartphones on memory and spatial information, both controlled by the hippocampus, are still being studied by many researchers, I have experienced joy in getting to know my neighborhood and the people living in it. The dumbphone experience amplifies the amount of human connection and bandwidth we possess while smart devices usually bent towards individualism. In practical terms, adapting to a low-tech lifestyle can involve sitting down with a physical or digital map to learn the routes needed for daily navigation. After a few weeks of practicing this skill, individuals will develop a stronger sense of their community, its surroundings, and how to get around.

Music

For many who transition to a voice-first device, a common concern is the absence of streaming platforms for music and video. Smartphones have conditioned us to expect unlimited streaming through apps, leading us to overlook simpler alternatives such as renting a DVD from a Redbox kiosk or purchasing a CD from a local store. With smartphones, we effortlessly log in, binge-watch or listen, and continue with our day. While a basic phone may not guarantee increased interaction with our surroundings or a happier life, it can prompt us to reevaluate how we acquire the items we desire. Unlike smartphones, which optimize apps for consumption and promote subscriptions or in-app purchases, basic phones encourage more deliberate decision-making and interaction with others. By visiting a record store, we create opportunities for engagement with the owner, cashier, or fellow customers seeking similar musical genres. In contrast, digital purchases often isolate us within our own spaces.

A study on the impact and resurgence of vinyl records by Dominik Bartmanski and Ian Woodard revealed that the tangible nature of vinyl records evokes feelings and memories in a way that digital media often cannot replicate. The physicality of records, with their cover art, liner notes, and tactile engagement, creates a more immersive and intimate listening experience. Furthermore, different audiences derive complex and multifaceted meanings from holding a physical record, which conveys layers of information to listeners. This emotional connection can foster a deeper appreciation for the music and the artists behind it. Bartmanski and Woodard noted that vinyl has the "ability to materialize a flexible range of meanings for its various audiences, with each pointing to a basic cultural structure which is anchored by notions of heritage, authenticity, and coolness."[9]

In this context, embracing simpler technologies, like basic phones or vinyl records, may not only alter our consumption patterns but also help us rediscover the value of meaningful connections, tangible experiences, and authentic interactions with the world around us. While some may view my experience as an anomaly, the return of vinyl represents a world of possibilities that can open up to us if we are willing to embrace friction in our lives. When it comes to music, we can create a deeper connection with our favorite music shops and artist by supporting them directly, rather than relying on meager royalties from streaming platforms like Spotify or Tidal. Not only does this direct support foster a more intimate relationship with the local owners, but it can also contribute to the financial development of our communities and enhance the music scene in our own neighborhoods. It's important to note that while individual decisions may not bring about seismic change, they can certainly have intrinsic positive effects that spread beyond our immediate circle. And on a more practical level, switching to a dedicated music or video player can greatly enhance our listening and viewing experiences. Whether it is physical records or mp3 players, curating a specific playlist will create a more intentional and personalized media library that truly resonates with us.

Communication Apps

A final concern for those considering the transition to minimal phones is the reliance on communication apps for work or family. In many parts of the world, instant messengers such as WhatsApp, Signal, or Line have become the default medium of communication. Similarly, email, Slack, and Microsoft Teams have become the dominant forces of interaction for remote and office workers. These platforms have revolutionized the way we communicate, allowing us to receive information promptly, securely, and on our own timeline. While the benefits of these resources cannot be denied, we must also acknowledge that they have created misalignment within our work and personal relationships.

Alicia Liu, in her Medium post titled "Death By a Thousand Pings: The Hidden Side of Using Slack," commented, "By lowering the barrier to initiate communication, the hidden side effect is that Slack has the quiet capacity to exponentially increase communication overhead, resulting in much more voluminous, lower quality communication."[10] The constant flow of messages can create an environment where focused work is diminished due to the need to constantly clarify information that is relayed back and forth, often causing miscommunication and confusion. This barrage of messages can lead to increased stress levels, as employees feel the pressure to constantly stay connected and respond immediately.

Moreover, Sarah Peck, founder and executive director of Startup Pregnant, an online community where people ask questions about parenting and entrepreneurship, said to a Vox reporter, "If we don't think critically about how we use the tools, we're going to be the same exact people in a new place. We won't be more or less efficient if we don't think critically about our choices around how we behave with the tool. We're just moving email to another place, and it's less searchable."[11] Peck's statement highlights the importance of not just adopting new tools, but also reevaluating our behavior and interaction with them. This involves setting boundaries and establishing best practices that prioritize quality communication and meaningful engagement. To improve the effectiveness of these communication tools, it is crucial to develop guidelines and strategies for their use within any type of organization. This may include setting designated hours for checking messages, creating dedicated channels for specific topics, and implementing a policy of addressing complex or sensitive issues through face-to-face or voice conversations. By being more mindful of how we use these platforms, we can create a balance between maintaining open lines of communication and fostering a productive, focused work environment that supports the well-being of all team members. This approach can help ensure that important conversations are not lost in the noise of digital chatter and that we maintain strong connections with our colleagues and loved ones.

As the end of the 2022 approached, I found myself knee-deep in the project of designing and organizing my organization's quarterly calendar. Being the head of the project, it was my responsibility to make sure that all the data from our volunteers was collected in a timely manner. I wanted to make things as easy as possible for everyone, so I made a variety of tools available to facilitate the input process. The advantages of using technology were obvious - it allowed us to be more efficient and sped up the entire process. However, as we began to use tools like WhatsApp, email, and text to communicate, problems arose. I noticed that my direct reports were feeling overwhelmed by the constant reminders and messages, which often came in at all hours of the day and night. They felt the need to respond instantly, rather than taking the time to collect their thoughts and get organized before submitting their information via the shared document I had created. It became clear to me that technology, while helpful, was also a source of stress and pressure. In my attempt to make things more efficient, I had become a disruptive force in my own organization.

Sitting at my desk, I felt uneasy as I realized that my leadership style was hindering productivity. I had inundated my team with a constant stream of emails, messages, and reminders that had become overwhelming. As the head of the quarterly calendar project for my organization, I had made several tools available for our volunteers to input their data, but I had failed to set clear expectations and boundaries for communication. Looking back at my behavior, I imagined myself in my team's shoes and wondered how I would feel. The constant reminders and delivery timelines repeated ad nauseam would have left me feeling disrespected and undervalued. I knew I had to change this, and so I turned once again to Cal Newport's book "A World Without Email." Newport talks about the hyperactive hive mind exhibited in apps like Slack, texts, or constant emails. He details how destructive communication behaviors demand people's attention almost instantly, causing unnecessary stress and anxiety.[12] It was clear that this approach was not working for my team, and I needed to re-think our communication strategy. I began to analyze how to best organize future requests for our leaders and volunteers, focusing on setting clear guidelines and boundaries to create a more productive and respectful work environment.

We spent several days exploring different communication models and eventually settled on a clear and concise strategy that would hold people accountable while still delivering results. Rather than bombarding our team with constant reminders and instant messages, we decided to send one email with clear deadlines and follow up with a scheduled phone call as a gentle reminder if someone was at risk of missing the scheduled dates. This small shift allowed us to trust our team members to complete their tasks while still maintaining accountability. As we approach Q2 2023, we're committed to delivering communication in a way that respects the valuable time and efforts of those who are dedicated to helping our organization thrive.

As the story reflects, our digital communication habits are far from perfect. The introduction of read receipts, delivered prompts, and replying functions has created a heightened level of expectations that were not present when we had to walk to our coworkers cubicle and ask for information. Though faster and reliable communication is a blessing, bending our time and attention toward the desires of our peers or colleagues can lead to a damaging conception of what's important and relevant to our lives. Living with a low tech outlook is an introduction to creating boundaries around our time and delivering clear expectations as to how we prefer to be reached out to.

A simple declaration to our family and friends that they will get a response in the next 24 hours accompanied by structured times for such responses will not only increase your time away from screens, but also give structure to how you engage with those that you love and care the most for.

So, should I purchase a dumbphone?

Absolutely! If you seek a slower-paced life complemented by mindful technology usage, a basic phone can support your pursuit of reduced consumption and enhanced connections. Phones with limited features inevitably introduce some challenges. However, these minor inconveniences are outweighed by the newfound freedom from sensory overload that becomes accessible. In Chapter 3, I will delve into the technical aspects of selecting a suitable dumbphone and discuss accompanying devices that can enrich the overall experience of a low-tech lifestyle.

Conversely, if the thought of a basic device lacking tap-to-pay, readily available maps, or Spotify seems too inconvenient, I encourage you to explore Chapter 4, where we will examine the concept of "transition devices." I use this term to describe phones that possess smartphone capabilities but, due to their form factor, are less addictive than their fully-fledged counterparts. While transition phones can be beneficial, it is important to remember that they still hold the potential for addiction and serve as a compromise rather than the complete lifestyle change I advocate for throughout this book.

---

1. Ghita, C., & Thorén, C. (2021). Going cold turkey! Digital detox experiences. Nordic Journal of Media Studies, 3(1), 161-164. https://doi.org/10.2478/nor-2021-0047
2. Clayton, R. B., Leshner, G., & Almond, A. (2015). The extended iSelf: The impact of iPhone separation on cognition, emotion, and physiology. Journal of Computer-Mediated Communication, 20(2), 119-135. DOI: 10.1111/jcc4.12109
3. Ibid.
4. Sen, K., Prybutok, G., & Prybutok, V. (2022). The use of digital technology for social wellbeing reduces social isolation in older adults: A systematic review. SSM-Population Health, 17, 101020. https://doi.org/10.1016/j.ssmph.2021.101020.

5. Zeng, Y., Zhang, J., Wei, J., & Li, S. (2022). The Impact of Undergraduates' Social Isolation on Smartphone Addiction: The Roles of Academic Anxiety and Social Media Use. International Journal of Environmental Research and Public Health, 19(23), 15903. https://doi.org/10.3390/ijerph192315903

Smartphone Addiction, Loneliness, Narcissistic Personality, and Family Belonging Among University Students: A Path Analysis

6. Comer, J. M. (2019). The Ruthless Elimination of Hurry: How to Stay Emotionally Healthy and Spiritually Alive in the Chaos of the Modern World. WaterBrook.
7. Dahmani, L., & Bohbot, V. D. (2020). Habitual use of GPS negatively impacts spatial memory during self-guided navigation. Scientific reports, 10(1), 6310. https://doi.org/10.1038/s41598-020-62877-0
8. Ishikawa, T., Fujiwara, H., Imai, O. & Okabe, A. (2008). Wayfinding with a GPS-based mobile navigation system: A comparison with maps and direct experience. Journal of Environmental Psychology, 28, 74–82. https://doi.org/10.1016/j.jenvp.2007.09.004

9. Bartmanski, D., & Woodward, I. (2015). The vinyl: The analogue medium in the age of digital reproduction. New media & society, 15(1), 132-148. https://doi.org/10.1177/1469540513488403
10. Liu, A. (2018, March 20). The Hidden Side of Using Slack. Counter-Intuition. https://medium.com/counter-intuition/the-hidden-side-of-using-slack-2443d9b66f8a
11. Molla, R. (2019, May 1). The productivity pit: how Slack is ruining work. Vox. https://www.vox.com/recode/2019/5/1/18511575/productivity-slack-google-microsoft-facebook
12. Newport, C. (2021). A World Without Email: Reimagining Work in an Age of Communication Overload. Portfolio/Penguin.

Chapter 3

I WANT A DUMBPHONE, BUT WHICH ONE?

As smartphones continue to become increasingly sophisticated, some individuals are seeking a return to the simplicity and basic functionality of a "dumbphone." However, choosing a dumbphone isn't as simple as it once was. Writer Kaitlyn Tiffany from The Atlantic found that the process of finding a phone that covers even the most basic needs is not a straightforward task. In her article, "Phones Will Never Be Fun Again," she wrote, "Shopping for such a device [a basic phone] today is hard. Walking into various stores in Brooklyn, I saw slabs, slabs, and more slabs. The only non-smartphones available at Target or Best Buy were super-cheap phones made explicitly for seniors (there were photos of old people on all of the boxes) or even cheaper burner phones made somewhat less explicitly for conducting criminal activity."[1] The lack of availability at local stores is just one factor to consider when choosing a dumbphone. Other critical considerations include carrier compatibility, software options, available features, and design preferences.

Carrier compatibility is the most crucial factor to consider when selecting a dumbphone, as not all basic phones are compatible with all carriers. Conducting thorough research is essential to identify a carrier that supports the specific model you want to use. In addition, software options for dumbphones can pose challenges. Some devices use proprietary operating systems, while others utilize modified versions of Android or other open-source systems. Another vital factor to consider is the available features of the phone. While some dumbphones offer only basic functions like texting and calling, others may include features like music players, cameras, and even basic internet browsing. It's important to determine which features matter to you and select a phone that meets your lifestyle. Finally, design and aesthetic preferences can also be a consideration when choosing a dumbphone. Some individuals may prefer a more minimalist look, while others may desire a phone with a unique design or color scheme. Ultimately, selecting a dumbphone comes down to personal preferences and priorities. By carefully considering these factors, you can choose a phone that aligns with your needs and lifestyle.

For those feeling overwhelmed by the technical aspects of selecting a dumbphone, the dumbphone finder is a valuable tool that can help. I created this website to offer an extensive list of LTE dumbphones with a range of features and specifications that can be filtered according to your preferences. Using this tool, you can quickly and easily locate a basic phone that meets your requirements, without the need to wade through technical discussions about carrier compatibility or software. The website also offers an intuitive interface that allows you to compare different models side by side, simplifying the decision-making process. Overall, the dumbphone finder is a fantastic resource for anyone considering a switch to a basic phone, particularly those new to the world of dumbphones who might feel overwhelmed by the technical language. You can visit the website at https://dumbphonefinder.com . If you want to learn more about the technical language surrounding dumbphones and gain a more in-depth understanding of the systems inside them, let's start with a primer!

Carrier Compatibility

My journey into the world of low-tech living began when I realized that my smartphone usage was spiraling out of control. I was constantly distracted by notifications, and my work productivity was suffering as a result. After conducting some research, I decided to take the plunge and find a more basic phone that would limit my access to the internet and social media, allowing me to regain control over my time and attention. Eager to make the transition during early 2019, I stumbled upon the Nokia Asha 301, a classic dumbphone with a reputation for its long battery life and user-friendly design. Without much thought, I ordered the device online and eagerly awaited its arrival.

When the package finally arrived, I excitedly unboxed the Nokia Asha 301 and attempted to insert my Verizon SIM card, only to realize that the phone was incompatible with my carrier's network. Frustrated and disappointed, I decided to dig deeper and understand the complexities of telecommunication networks to avoid making the same mistake again. My research revealed that networks in North America have evolved significantly over the years, with carriers like Verizon, AT&T, and T-Mobile phasing out older 2G and 3G networks in favor of more advanced 4G and 5G technology. This technological shift had rendered many older devices, like the Nokia Asha 301, obsolete and incompatible with modern networks.

As I delved further into the world of telecommunication devices, I learned about the importance of LTE bands and operating systems in ensuring compatibility between a device and a carrier. I discovered that some carriers use specific LTE bands, and understanding which bands are supported by your carrier is crucial in selecting a compatible device. Furthermore, I realized that older operating systems, once popular on Nokia, Motorola, and Palm devices, were no longer able to function on current networks.

Armed with this newfound knowledge, I began my search anew, focusing on finding a dumbphone that was compatible with my carrier's network and met my requirements for a more minimalist lifestyle. Eventually, I discovered the perfect device for me that allowed me to limit my access to the internet and social media, enabling me to reclaim my time, focus, and productivity.

My experience in navigating the world of low-tech living taught me the importance of understanding the intricacies of telecommunication networks and devices. By learning about key terms, such as LTE bands and operating systems, I was able to make an informed decision and find a suitable device that met my needs, ultimately enhancing my quality of life. If you're looking to switch to a low tech lifestyle, one of the first things you'll need to consider is whether your phone is compatible with your provider of choice. The easiest way to do this is to follow your provider's approved devices list or confirm which LTE bands are compatible with their service. For example, the Light Phone 2 possesses LTE bands B2, B4, B12, B13, B17, B25, and B26, which overlap with multiple carriers in the United States and abroad, but not all.

To ensure that your phone will work with your provider's LTE bands, a good first step is to do a simple search with your provider to see what bands they provide. Additionally, Cellmapper.net in the United States is a fantastic resource that can help you understand the location and bands of the towers around you. By using their website tool, you can gain insight into the specific frequency bands that are being used by nearby cell towers, as well as their exact location. Once you have identified which LTE bands your provider uses, you can cross-reference this information with your preferred phone to ensure that it will work with their service. These two steps will save you a headache when trying to find which phones work with the best provider in your area.

Overall, taking the time to research LTE bands and ensure that your phone is compatible with your provider can help to ensure a smooth and stress-free transition to a low tech lifestyle. With the help of resources like Cellmapper.net and your provider's approved devices list, you can make informed decisions about your phone and enjoy a more mindful and intentional relationship with technology.

Another crucial aspect to consider when choosing a phone compatible with your desired network is determining whether the device is unlocked or not. Network-unlocked devices with suitable bands typically cause fewer issues when using your preferred SIM card. Most devices sold outside North America are network-unlocked, simplifying compatibility for those in Europe, Africa, or Latin America. However, factors such as government regulations, telecom providers, and exclusive contracts between manufacturers and carriers make devices sold in the United States and Canada more likely to be network-locked and face compatibility challenges. Take the TCL Flip 2 as an example. Retailing at $20, this device meets many basic phone requirements and offers an excellent user experience. However, it is locked to Tracfone unless you activate it, use one of their plans for 60 days, and then request an unlock code. Afterward, it is only compatible with a limited number of carriers due to their "approved devices list" or "whitelisting" procedures (specifically, AT&T and Verizon). Users often have to negotiate with telecom companies to activate compatible devices, even after ensuring proper LTE band support.

One final aspect to examine regarding carrier compatibility involves MVNOs (Mobile Virtual Network Operators). These companies lease network infrastructure from major providers and offer their services at lower prices, catering to budget-conscious consumers. Typically, MVNOs forgo premium features or promotions to provide essential services similar to those offered by leading carriers. For example, Mint Mobile, owned by Ryan Reynolds, utilizes T-Mobile's network and delivers service to its customers at a fraction of the cost. Instead of paying $40 to $60 to T-Mobile, Mint Mobile subscribers pay $15 for comparable coverage as postpaid customers. Other notable MVNOs include Cricket Wireless, which operates on AT&T's network, and US Mobile, which uses both Verizon's and T-Mobile's network. MVNOs are particularly relevant to the dumbphone conversation, as they tend to be more accommodating in allowing a wider range of devices on their networks than major carriers. This open attitude benefits basic phone enthusiasts since older devices can still function in certain areas. Consequently, exploring MVNOs' cost-effective plans and flexible device requirements is worthwhile if your preferred carrier does not support your chosen dumbphone. Additionally, MVNOs often provide simple, easy-to-understand plans, making them ideal for those seeking a no-frills experience. They may also offer pay-as-you-go or prepaid options, giving users more control over their mobile expenses.

Having delved into the intricacies of network bands, grasped the role and advantages of Mobile Virtual Network Operators (MVNOs), and become acquainted with the process of network unlocks, it's time to direct our attention to other critical factors in choosing the perfect dumbphone. Among these factors are the operating systems, hardware specifications, and additional features that can influence your decision. In this section, we will explore the various operating systems available for dumbphones, discussing their unique characteristics, strengths, and weaknesses. This information will be instrumental in helping you identify which system aligns with your preferences and low-tech lifestyle goals.

Operating Systems

Since the early 2000s, the cell phone software landscape has undergone significant changes. Numerous operating systems have emerged and vanished, struggling to keep pace with rapidly evolving technology. Windows Mobile, Blackberry, Symbian, Meego, and Firefox OS are some examples of operating systems that lost market share and eventually disappeared. In the last decade, Android and iOS have risen as the dominant forces in the smartphone market. Android, developed by Google, has become the most widely used smartphone operating system, boasting over 2.5 billion active devices worldwide. It offers a vast array of features and can be customized by manufacturers to meet their specific needs. In contrast, iOS, developed by Apple, enjoys popularity among Apple device users for its streamlined user experience and communication apps like iMessage and FaceTime. However, the dumbphone market features additional operating systems apart from Android. KaiOS, ThreadX, and MuditaOS are three actively developed dumbphone operating systems. KaiOS, a descendant of Firefox OS, has gained popularity in recent years, particularly in emerging markets. ThreadX is an embedded system developed from Azure technologies, while MuditaOS is an independent operating system created by Mudita. Despite Android's commanding market share of around 85%, the demand for dumbphones running KaiOS, ThreadX, and MuditaOS continues to grow.

Basic phones, such as the Light Phone 2, Punkt MP02, and Sunbeam F1, provide a simpler alternative to smartphones. These devices offer essential phone features like calling and texting without the added complexities of smartphones. Nevertheless, even basic phones like these frequently use Android as their base layer. Manufacturers customize these devices to remove Google services and implement their own privacy-optimized basic tools. LightOS, AphyOS, and BasicOS, for instance, are built and customized from a minimalistic version of the Android Open Source Project and modified to align with each company's philosophy. Although not ideal, Android remains the only operating system that effectively works with LTE bands, chipset configurations, and allows phone makers to create these phones. It is crucial to note that these basic phones still rely on a downsized smart operating system to fit the flip or candy bar form factor. While they offer a more straightforward and privacy-focused option, the compromises made in using Android may not appeal to those seeking a semi-2000s experience.

Developing a new operating system for basic phones can be a challenging and costly endeavor for companies. MuditaOS has spearheaded the development of a new basic system but has encountered significant obstacles. Their features occasionally clash with LTE bands across countries, the music tool cannot play in the background, and their tethering interface's reliability remains uncertain. Until companies prioritize developing their own operating systems and market adoption for these alternatives increases, various customizations of Android will continue to be the most viable solution for bringing basic phones to low-tech enthusiasts.

One of the primary advantages of using a dumbphone is the enhanced privacy it offers compared to smartphones. Due to their limited storage space, dumbphones present fewer opportunities for data collection. Unlike smartphones, feature phones are less likely to store personal data, such as emails, messages, and photos. Consequently, even if your phone is lost or stolen, there is less information that can be accessed by a third party. Moreover, most dumbphones do not sync and store data between your phone and a server, thereby reducing the amount of personal data that can be collected. With fewer apps than smartphones, dumbphones also have fewer opportunities for apps to gather data about you. Many smartphone apps collect data like your location, browsing history, and contacts, which can be used for targeted advertising or sold to third-party companies. By using a feature phone, you can decrease the amount of personal data collected about you and regain control over your online privacy.

Another privacy benefit of using a dumbphone is its decreased vulnerability to phishing attacks and malware.

Owing to their limited capabilities, feature phones generally lack the advanced web browsers and email clients found on smartphones. This prevents them from running scripts or downloading attachments containing malware or other malicious software. Furthermore, the simplistic operating systems of dumbphones make them less appealing targets for hackers, providing an added layer of security for users concerned about their online privacy. However, one drawback of using a dumbphone is the unavailability of encrypted communication apps like Signal or Session, which provide end-to-end encryption to safeguard messages from interception and decoding. Despite this limitation, important and sensitive information can still be securely exchanged through desktop clients for encrypted messaging, ensuring privacy.

In summary, feature phones and voice-first phones provide users with increased privacy and security by collecting less data and being less attractive targets for hackers. This results in a lower likelihood of users falling victim to cyberattacks or having their personal information compromised. These devices cater to those who wish to simplify their communication experience, reduce daily screen time, and focus more on face-to-face interactions. When choosing an operating system for your dumbphone, it is essential to consider factors such as your daily activities, privacy concerns, and ease of use. The ideal operating system should align with your needs and preferences while minimizing distractions and intrusion into your personal life. By carefully evaluating the available options, you can find a dumbphone that strikes the right balance between functionality and simplicity, ultimately enhancing your communication experience while protecting your privacy and security.

What makes a dumbphone a dumbphone?

The ongoing debate about what truly defines a dumbphone is rooted in the perception and expectations of the device's capabilities. While some people believe that a dumbphone should only support basic calls and texts, it's essential to recognize that even early cellphones from the 2000s featured calendars, web browsers, and music players. Though these features were relatively basic and slow to load, they still provided users with a range of functionalities, such as games, apps, and other services. As smartphones have become increasingly dominant, the perception of dumbphones has devolved, leading many to assume that these devices should be outdated and offer only a limited set of features.

The current market offers a diverse array of devices, ranging from those that only support basic calls and texts to those that incorporate a few modern features. Android-based devices are particularly adaptable, as they can be customized to include a selection of smart apps while limiting access to infinite content feeds. Moreover, KaiOS-powered devices can run some useful apps, albeit with software constraints that prevent overly complex functionality. For example, the Nokia 2780, a KaiOS 3.0 device, can run a podcast app, display weather updates, and provide a stripped-down version of Google Maps for convenience. However, it does not allow unrestricted access to platforms like Reddit, Discord, or other social networks. Another minimalist phone, the Nokia 2720, enables users to access podcasts and WhatsApp, but its browser struggles to handle web streaming services or load articles efficiently.

On the Android side of things, the Sunbeam F1 can manage your calendar, store MP3 files, and send voice-to-text messages, but it does not include a browser or any additional apps. Moreover, the Light Phone 2 team has developed a guiding ethos for their platform, LightOS, which dictates the inclusion of specific tools within the phone. The current offerings include features such as podcasts, calendars, directions, music, and notes. However, the Light Phone 2 deliberately excludes access to algorithm-based services designed to capture your attention and keep you glued to the screen. The team has stated that email, Facebook, or browsers that foster user dependency will not be added to the phone. In line with their slogan, the Light Phone 2 is intended to be "used as little as possible." The critical distinction between basic phones and transition devices lies in their respective capabilities, and it is essential to consider these differences when choosing a device that best suits your everyday living and work needs.

In my perspective, dumbphones should be designed with simplicity as their core principle, featuring only limited app capabilities and intentionally excluding high-spec features such as high-resolution cameras, high-refresh LCD touchscreens, or vast amounts of RAM memory. The primary focus of these devices is to facilitate genuine connections with loved ones and the world around you, rather than acting as a constant gateway to the internet. Cal Newport, in his book Digital Minimalism, sheds light on this philosophy: "Digital minimalists see new technologies as tools to be used to support things they deeply value—not as sources of value themselves. They don't accept the idea that offering some small benefit is justification for allowing an attention-gobbling service into their lives and are instead interested in applying new technology in highly selective and intentional ways that yield big wins. Just as important: they're comfortable missing out on everything else."[2]

This mindset encourages a more intentional approach to technology, where users of dumbphones can utilize essential features without becoming overwhelmed or distracted by unnecessary apps and services. These devices may include essential tools such as a basic browser, alarm clocks, and local calendars, but these features are primarily designed for quick-reference purposes. In contrast to smartphones, dumbphones are not intended to lure users down a rabbit hole of endless, algorithmically-generated content. By limiting the available features, dumbphones enable users to focus on what truly matters in their lives, fostering a healthier relationship with technology. This approach to device design encourages users to live more in the present moment and engage more deeply with their surroundings, promoting a more fulfilling and balanced life.

Recommendations

When delving into the realm of dumbphones and basic devices, it's crucial to consider aspects such as long-term support, communication, and the manufacturers' dedication to their products. Switching to a low-tech phone is often viewed as a step towards an improved quality of life. Therefore, selecting a device from a company that is committed to its product, provides timely updates, and offers support for hardware or software issues can ensure a smooth and enjoyable transition to a low-tech lifestyle. As a Light Phone 2 enthusiast, I have personally experienced the company's unwavering commitment to their product. Nevertheless, it's important to recognize that the Light Phone 2 may not be the ideal choice for everyone, as individual needs and preferences vary.

Various alternatives exist in the dumbphone market, with my recommendations focusing on long-term support and communication. Both Sunbeam and Light excel in this area, making their devices, Sunbeam F1 and Light Phone 2, well rounded choices. The Sunbeam F1 offers a minimalist design and essential functionalities, striking a balance between simplicity and functionality. The Light Phone 2, designed for intentional technology use, features a sleek e-ink display and a focused set of tools. Both devices come highly recommended for users seeking a more intentional and low-tech lifestyle. While their products might carry a higher price tag compared to some basic phones, they are proactive in providing updates and keeping their customers satisfied. The adage "you get what you pay for" certainly rings true in the dumbphone space. On the other hand, Nokia devices, now produced by HMD Global, have not maintained the same degree of commitment. The company tends to revive old classics like the Nokia 225 or Nokia 8210 with 4G chipsets for compatibility with current standards, only to seemingly neglect them until the next release cycle. Although these affordable devices may be tempting for some, potential buyers should weigh the lack of support and assistance from the manufacturer when making their decision.

For those on a tighter budget, the TCL Flip 2 and LG Classic are excellent alternatives in the dumbphone market. Both devices concentrate on core communication functionality, providing exceptional call and texting experiences that surpass what Nokia phones can deliver. The TCL Flip 2, a modern interpretation of the classic flip phone design, features a compact form factor perfect for users who appreciate the convenience of a small, pocketable device. The LG Classic, a flip phone that merges a classic design with modern features, offers a straightforward, no-frills communication experience. If needed, both of these devices can be further customized to include one or two extra apps, with resources like https://apps4flip.com providing guides on adding useful features. While they may not be the most visually appealing devices on the market, they offer wide compatibility and can be found in similar versions across multiple countries worldwide.

Another intriguing segment in the dumbphone market is kosher phones. Designed with the Jewish community in mind, these heavily restricted devices feature only approved apps. While they exclude social media and infinite feeds, kosher phones often include calendars, music players, and occasionally Waze or Uber. Although some might not categorize them as "dumbphones" in the traditional sense, they deliver a non-addictive and low-tech experience. You can find the latest offerings on websites like https://koshercell.org, which provide updates on this type of device. As a reminder, to assist in your search for the perfect device, the dumbphone finder offers links, network compatibility information, and feature filters on all these devices. I have just offered some guidelines and a sample of devices that are from my recommendation list. The dumbphone finder will guide you to the best purchasing options and help you stay updated on the features and support services offered by the manufacturers. It has a "Jose's rating" category where you can find my updated recommendations and thoughts on these devices.

Now that we've covered minimal and basic devices, it's time to delve into the world of transition devices and understand how they can complement a low-tech lifestyle. These unique devices strike a balance between the simplicity of dumbphones and the advanced capabilities of smartphones, catering to individuals seeking a more intentional and mindful approach to technology. In the next chapter, we will explore the various transition devices available on the market, highlighting their key features and discussing the advantages they provide for users looking to maintain a low-tech lifestyle without sacrificing the essential conveniences of modern technology.

---

1. Tiffany, K. (2023, April 5). Phones Will Never Be Fun Again. The Atlantic. https://www.theatlantic.com/technology/archive/2023/04/dumb-phone-trend-light-phone-punkt-sunbeam/673663/

2. Newport, C. (2019). Digital minimalism: Choosing a focused life in a noisy world. Penguin.

Chapter 4

I DON'T WANT A DUMBPHONE, BUT MY SCREENTIME IS AWFUL!

I can still vividly recall that day. The skies were clear, and a gentle breeze rustled the leaves outside my window as I eagerly sat down to watch the Apple event. As the presentation unfolded and the new "Screen Time" feature was announced, I felt a surge of hope swelling in my chest. I genuinely believed that this new iPhone update would help me overcome my addiction to YouTube and Reddit, putting an end to the countless hours I had wasted on my device. My heart raced as I downloaded the update, meticulously setting up limits for my two most problematic apps, and basking in the satisfaction of finally taking control of my digital habits. But as the sun set and rose again, bringing forth a new day, I quickly realized that my excitement was short-lived. Within just 24 hours, I stumbled upon a glaring flaw in the Screen Time feature: it was all too easy to bypass the restrictions with a couple of taps. The first prompt innocently asked if I needed more time, while the second temptingly offered to disable my self-imposed limits for the rest of the day. My initial enthusiasm was replaced by a sinking feeling of disappointment, as I understood that the onus was still on me to resist the allure of endless content.

Apple's Screen Time feature, initially hailed as a helpful tool for managing phone use, had proven to be less effective than anticipated. While the feature aimed to set boundaries on device usage, it appears that its ultimate goal may have been to encourage users to engage more with Apple's platform, thereby boosting corporate profits or the like. In a 2019 Wall Street Journal article, Reed Albergotti revealed an unsurprising reality: "kids are outsmarting an army of engineers from Cupertino, Calif., home to Apple's headquarters in Silicon Valley." The parental discovery led to concerns about the ease with which children could bypass Screen Time restrictions, using platforms like Reddit and YouTube to share knowledge and techniques for defeating the feature. Some parents commented about the disappointment that a company that had promised a real solution to their kids addiction wouldn't be very responsive to the exploits shared in online forums. As a result, many children were able to continue the very behaviors their parents sought to curtail. Child psychologist Adam Pletter highlighted in the same piece the potential danger of Apple's service, stating that it can create a false sense of security among parents who believe they are effectively monitoring their children's device usage.[1]

Even for adults, Screen Time has proven to be less than foolproof. The feature can be exploited and disabled by users looking to avoid limitations on unhelpful or time-wasting apps. While apps like Screen Time may provide some utility in tracking one's smartphone usage, they seem to fall short in their primary goal: to help users reduce the time they spend in front of screens. As Laura Zimmerman noted in her research, despite the promise of these applications, they often fail to deliver meaningful reductions in phone use. They serve as the means to keep track of your usage, but will not make a dent in creating healthier habits.[2] As the days turned into weeks, my issue of constant screen access merely evolved into a series of easily bypassable nudges and reminders. The result remained the same: I spent countless hours on my device, my attention held hostage by the digital world, while my Master's papers lay abandoned on my desk. During this crucial period of my life, I found myself questioning my ability to break free from the invisible chains tethering me to my phone. It was during one of those introspective moments that I remembered a situation from my time in Berrien Springs that echoed my own struggle. The town had been buzzing with excitement when local politicians announced the implementation of a bike lane, touting it as a means to promote eco-friendly transportation. With great fanfare, the project was completed, and the bike lane stretched invitingly along the streets, encouraging residents to choose a healthier, greener way to commute.

However, when winter arrived, and snow blanketed the roads of the town, the shortcomings of this initiative became apparent. The bike lane, now buried beneath a thick layer of snow, lay abandoned and unusable. No one took responsibility for clearing the path, and the once-promising solution to reducing pollution and promoting healthy living turned into another example of an incomplete effort. This situation in Berrien Springs served as a stark reminder that simply creating a solution is not enough – there must be a genuine commitment to see it through, and ensure that it is effective in achieving its intended goal. Much like the bike lane, the Screen Time feature on my iPhone had become an incomplete solution, placing the onus on me, rather than truly helping me achieve the goal to leave endless content aside.

Size Matters

As we delve deeper into the concept of transition devices, it's important to understand that they are not designed to serve as a digital detox. Instead, transition devices are meant to be the first step in a larger transformation towards a digitally balanced lifestyle. If you approach these devices solely as a means to detox from the internet, they may provide temporary relief, but lasting change may be difficult to achieve, as you are only using them for a limited period. Transition devices are intended to serve as an intermediate stage on the journey towards digital wellbeing. They often feature smaller or alternative form factors that create friction for users while retaining enough smart features to alleviate anxiety and maintain essential functionality.

To illustrate the importance of size and form factor, I'd like to share a personal story about my struggle with weight management over the past decade. I have always had a passion for food and enjoy indulging in well-prepared meals. Dining out, I would order appetizers, main dishes, and desserts to satisfy my cravings and make the most of the experience. At home, I aimed to create meals that would delight my palate. In the first chapter, I discussed the lifestyle changes I made regarding exercise and food intake. Now, I want to share the single factor that has had the most significant impact on my journey towards healthier eating habits: the size of my plate.

Growing up in Nicaragua, my mother prepared amazing meals with simple ingredients that were always rich in flavor. The size of my plate, however, remained constant throughout my formative years. With an 8-inch diameter, my plate could only hold so much food. I loved my mom's cooking, but the portions were just enough for the day – nothing more, nothing less. Upon moving to the United States, I was astonished by the size of "regular" plates, which averaged 12 inches in diameter – 50% larger than those in other parts of the world. It's no wonder that issues with weight management and related diseases are prevalent in America, given the enormity of our food and drink containers compared to the rest of the world. A "medium" soft drink in U.S. food halls would be considered extra-large elsewhere. Size indeed matters when it comes to consumption.

As a study on the effect of screen size when viewing Netflix reveals, participants who used "the small 4.5-inch phone screen recorded the lowest immersion scores, and there was a significant main effect of screen size on immersion scores when compared to both the 13-inch laptop and 30-inch monitor screens." Participants who used larger screens were further grasped by the experience than those who had smaller sized devices.[3] Over the past decade, smartphones have undergone a significant transformation, with screen size being a notable aspect of change. Since 2012, iPhones and Android devices have consistently increased in screen size, from the early models with a 3.5-inch display to the latest models boasting 5.5-inch and larger screens. I still recall the release of the Galaxy Note, featuring a massive screen and body with a stylus, which was the first of its kind in the market. While the large screen was appealing for consuming content, the overall size was cumbersome and challenged the notion of a phone's portability. During this time period, people stuck to their 3.5 to 4 inch screens instead of succumbing to the gargantuan form factor.

However, fast forward 10 years, and companies have managed to fit larger displays into slimmer, bezel-less devices, which have become increasingly popular among customers. The larger screens have enabled a more immersive experience, increasing the interaction between customers and their devices, thereby creating a more intimate relationship between people and technology. As a result, people are more drawn to their phones, often at the expense of engaging with the world around them. The screen size of smartphones has become an important factor in customer satisfaction, and companies are investing heavily in research and development to improve the screen-to-body ratio and overall display quality. While larger screens may enhance the user experience, they can also lead to negative consequences, such as eye strain and a decreased ability to focus on real-world tasks. Therefore, it is important to find a balance between the advantages of larger screens and the need to disconnect from technology and engage with the world.

Transition devices, then, can be a helpful tool in our efforts to reevaluate and adjust our relationship with technology. These devices, with their smaller screens or flip-style design, encourage users to focus on essential communication functions while leaving more robust tasks to laptops, tablets, or desktop computing devices. This separation creates a need for planning instead of constantly consuming digital content throughout the day. Just as smaller plates can assist with weight management, opting for devices with more manageable form factors can create a natural barrier against overconsumption, helping us strike a healthier balance between our digital and real-world lives. As you prepare to make a selection for your low-tech lifestyle, keep in mind that the size and form of the device you choose will impact how often and how you use it.

Design Matters

I love sipping coffee in the morning. The ritual of preparing it with my pour-over set and savoring each sip from my favorite cup is incredibly enjoyable. Yet, I never realized that my love for morning coffee wasn't just about the taste. The design and feel of the cup play a significant role in my experience. Numerous studies have explored people's attachment to physical objects, covering topics from hoarding behaviors to the idea that learning is best achieved through tangible interactions. In a study published by the Educational Psychology Review, Magdalena Novak and Stepahn Schwan investigated whether haptic feedback enhances the learning experience. After trials and different experiments, the study found that haptic exploration of real objects can contribute to the formation of enriched mental representations, supporting the acquisition of biologically primary and secondary knowledge. These two researchers noted that participants who engaged with objects had a deeper ability to recall than those that were only able to see the objects from the exhibits.[4] The underlying principle is clear: we develop an affinity for the design and physicality of our possessions. The more attractive they are or our simple ability to engage with them makes a stronger our bond between them and us.

Similarly, a second concern with the current state of smartphones is their design. Cellphones from the past had quirky designs, keyboards, and basic materials. They were functional devices serving utilitarian purposes such as communication, coordination, and basic reminders. Losing an old Nokia might have upset you for a day, but it didn't contain sensitive information like credit card details or personal journal entries. Your old phone was just a phone, perhaps with an added alarm clock function. In contrast, smartphones have not only increased in price due to their sleek and captivating designs but also created an immersive experience that melds software and hardware to hold our attention. Nowadays, people are increasingly reporting higher levels of nomophobia (no mobile phone phobia) in different parts of the world. As a recent systematic review on the topic has pointed out, "The prevalence of severe nomophobia is approximately 21% in the general adult population."[5] While these figures are rough estimates, and we are still learning about the consequences of continued smartphone use on our psyche, it's evident that anxiety related to smartphone dependence is far beyond anecdotes shared among friends.[6]

The increasing dominance of smartphones in our lives has become a growing concern as they become more advanced and captivating. Companies like Apple and Google continue to design phones that are sleek and easy to use, but their underlying purpose is to keep users hooked on their devices. Smartphones are designed to constantly stimulate us, creating a need for instant gratification and making it hard to put them down. These devices are not designed to help us reach our full potential but rather to keep us distracted and addicted to their features. As Shoshana Zuboff aptly states, "We are no longer the subjects of value realization. Nor are we, as some have insisted, the 'product' of Google's sales. Instead, we are the objects from which raw materials are extracted and expropriated for Google's prediction factories. Predictions about our behavior are Google's products, and they are sold to its actual customers but not to us. We are the means to others' ends."[7]

The addictive nature of smartphones is having a detrimental effect on our well-being, with a growing body of evidence suggesting that excessive smartphone use can lead to anxiety, depression, and poor sleep quality.[8] The devices are designed to keep us constantly engaged, to make it hard for us to put them down, and to keep our attention away from the real world. They are a source of distraction from work, friends, and family, taking away our time and preventing us from living in the present moment. These are all deliberate design choices. While smartphones have become tools for our distraction, companies could prioritize well-being instead of user exploitation. As a society, we need to become more aware of the detrimental effects of excessive smartphone use and demand greater accountability from the companies that create them. Instead of being passive consumers of technology, we must become more active participants in shaping our relationship with these devices, using them in a way that empowers us to reach our full potential rather than inhibits it.

There is a reason why we have a heightened experience when we consume hot drinks in porcelain cups instead of paper ones from Starbucks. The container itself makes a difference. Its design evokes a distinct feeling when we place our lips on it to drink tea, coffee, or hot chocolate. A porcelain cup is meant to be cherished and reused, not discarded after a single use. Similarly, the design of the devices we choose to accompany us on our life journey should be intentional. We must understand the purpose behind their creation and consider if, and how, they genuinely enhance our human experience.

Reduce, Replace, Reframe.

One of the solutions to the size and design conundrums can be found in transition devices. The content inside of the device is not the main issue; rather, it is the container and the way it was designed. Similar to how people enjoy watching a blockbuster movie at the theater instead of on their phones, we can retain some of the conveniences of the online world while placing them in devices that respect our time and attention.

    The CAT S22 Flip is an example of such a device. With its flip phone form factor, it may not be the most appealing in terms of design. It is bulky, heavy, and has suboptimal screen resolution and viewing angles. However, the device still has access to all the tools smartphones do, such as transit applications, email, Slack, and even Zoom. Thanks to its smart operating system, this flip phone acts as an intermediary in the de-digitalization process. It allows users to interact with the online world, but only to a limited extent. The experience of composing a message via the physical T9 keyboard or the tiny low-resolution touchscreen is unlikely to draw people to spend hours on end in front of it. Watching a video, although technically possible, won't be the same as enjoying it on a smartphone screen. This is why it's called a transition device. It has smart features, but the experience encourages users to utilize other devices while sitting at a terminal or enjoying a movie at the theater.

Transition devices, however, can also become a source of transferring your problems. While initially they may serve as a step towards decluttering your life and slowing down, they suffer some of the drawbacks of smartphones. If you customize them to fit your current lifestyle with multiple apps, services, and providers, you may end up frustrated, as they are definitely less advanced than their full-screen counterparts. Therefore, it is crucial to reframe their usage and establish boundaries, as you would with a smart device.

The initial step in reframing your use of electronics involves recognizing the challenges and the need for a change. Years of reliance on screens have made it difficult for us to imagine life without constant digital connectivity. However, a willingness to introspect and critically assess our habits can help us identify areas where we can reduce our dependence on electronic devices. This exercise requires patience and determination, but it is essential for striking a balance between our digital and analog lives. As you begin to reevaluate your relationship with electronics, start by determining which tasks can be delegated to analog products instead of relying solely on digital devices. For example, consider using a paper-based personal calendar to manage your schedule or a physical journal to jot down your tasks. This approach allows you to oversee your time on a larger timescale and visualize your commitments without the distractions and interruptions that digital screens often bring. Once you have set up your analog calendar, use digital alternatives only as a backup, reinforcing the primary role of the analog system in your scheduling process.

Another way to prioritize analog products is by integrating them into your daily routines. Replace your phone's alarm with a physical alarm clock, which can be particularly beneficial in creating a healthy sleep environment. By using an old-fashioned alarm clock, you can remove the temptation to check your phone immediately upon waking up, allowing you to start your day with a sense of calm and focus, free from the dopamine rush triggered by notifications and messages. Finally, be mindful of your overall screen time and make a conscious effort to engage in activities that do not involve electronic devices. Spend time with friends and family, engage in physical activities, or pick up a hobby that encourages you to disconnect from the digital world. As you cultivate these habits and establish boundaries for your electronic usage, you will find a healthier balance between your digital and analog lives, ultimately enhancing your overall well-being and quality of life.

Numerous other examples demonstrate the effectiveness of the reduce, replace, reframe principle. Almost everyone has an app they believe they can't live without.

However, as you become more adept at minimizing your reliance on digital sources for work, family, or other matters, you'll discover that adopting a lifestyle reminiscent of the pre-digital era is still feasible today. All it requires is intentionality and thoughtful planning.

Recommendations

If you're considering transition devices, I recommend starting with your current smartphone. You might be puzzled since this discussion revolves around low-tech solutions, and smartphones don't typically fall into that category. However, throughout my three years of assisting people in reducing screen time, I've found that the majority of those seeking transition devices benefit most from imposing strict limitations on their existing smartphones. If that approach proves ineffective, then it's time to consider changing the device's form factor. There are several powerful tools that can transform your smartphone into a more basic experience.

For iOS devices, there are a few notable software limitations. First, Unpluq is an app that allows you to set intentions and limitations for the apps you want to use. It requires that you either tap a physical object to access apps for a 5-minute period or use one of their software tricks to unlock the apps you have locked down. Although I have discussed previously that Screen Time is not as effective, giving the password to a significant other or loved one may be enough for you. Parental controls, although they can be bypassed, may be another alternative to address your software concerns. Finally, apps like OneSec or Clearspace introduce a delay in the interaction between apps, allowing you to make a conscious decision to use your phone or not. Pairing these software tools with other simplifying ideas like deleting all unnecessary apps or completely getting rid of them from your home screen can provide some relief to those struggling with obsessive smartphone use.

Android smartphones offer even more customization options. In addition to apps that can limit your usage like Unpluq or OneSec, you can use the Android Debug Bridge (ADB) through a laptop or the web to uninstall distracting apps from your device. Tools like ADB App Control or Web Adb enable users to create a tailored version of any Android phone. You can delete almost everything from the phone, including Google apps and preinstalled software, and leave it only with the productivity apps you want. However, if these measures seem simplistic and insufficient in addressing smartphone design and size concerns, that's because they are. While they may benefit those truly committed to a simpler lifestyle, touchscreens and other features in smartphones can entice users through object association. For those struggling with screen time, a flip phone or a different device altogether might be more effective.

For an updated list of devices that I recommend, make sure to visit the dumbphone finder. As of this writing, phones like the Kyocera DuraXV, CAT S22 Flip, and Jelly 2 offer designs and sizes that limit usage to the essentials and nothing more. These devices boast the broadest app compatibility, and their manufacturers are dedicated to providing regular updates. Outside the North American market, options like the Opel Touch Flip and the Xiaomi F21 line cater to customers in Asia, Oceania, and Europe. As always, it's essential to verify these devices' compatibility in your region and determine whether they align with the lifestyle you aim to cultivate.

---

1. Reed Albergotti. (2019, October 15). Teens find circumventing Apple's parental controls is child's play. The Washington Post. https://www.washingtonpost.com/technology/2019/10/15/teens-find-circumventing-apples-parental-controls-is-childs-play/
2. Zimmermann, L. (2021). "'Your screen-time app is keeping track': consumers are happy to monitor but unlikely to reduce smartphone usage." Journal of the Association for Consumer Research, 6(3), 377-382. https://doi.org/10.1086/714365

3. Rigby, J. M., Brumby, D. P., Cox, A. L., & Gould, S. J. J. (2016). Watching Movies on Netflix: Investigating the Effect of Screen Size on Viewer Immersion. In Proceedings of the 18th International Conference on Human-Computer Interaction with Mobile Devices and Services Adjunct (pp. 714-721). Association for Computing Machinery. https://doi.org/10.1145/2957265.2961843

4. Novak, M., Schwan, S. (2021). Does Touching Real Objects Affect Learning?. Educational Psychology Review, 33(3), 637-665. https://doi.org/10.1007/s10648-020-09551-z

5. Humood, A., Altooq, N., Altamimi, A., Almoosawi, H., Alzafiri, M., Bragazzi, N. L., Husni, M., & Jahrami, H. (2021). The prevalence of nomophobia by population and by research tool: A systematic review, meta-analysis, and meta-regression. Psych, 3(2), 249-258. https://doi.org/10.3390/psych3020019

6. Bhattacharya, S., Bashar, M. A., Srivastava, A., & Singh, A. (2019). NOMOPHOBIA: NO MObile PHone PhoBIA. Journal of Family Medicine and Primary Care, 8(4), 1297–1300. https://doi.org/10.4103/jfmpc.jfmpc_71_19

7. Zuboff, S. (2019). The Age of Surveillance Capitalism: The Fight for a Human Future at the New Frontier of Power. PublicAffairs.

8. Yao, N., Wang, Q. (2022). Technostress from Smartphone Use and Its Impact on University Students' Sleep Quality and Academic Performance. Asia-Pacific Education Researcher. https://doi.org/10.1007/s40299-022-00654-5

Chapter 5

Mastering Boredom

There's no scientific data to support this, but I'm quite sure that the phrase most often spoken by children is, "I'm bored." As someone who has worked with kids and teenagers from various backgrounds over the past seven years, I've heard this declaration so frequently that I've learned to bear it, no matter how exasperating it may be. I can't deny that, when I was young, I also used that phrase quite a bit. I remember how my mother would dread taking long car rides with me. My restless mind would constantly search for something to entertain itself, whether it was playing games, counting the cars that passed us by, or incessantly changing the FM radio stations because I couldn't bear listening to the classical concertos and sonatas that the local station broadcasted. Like most children, my brain sought new and exciting stimuli to keep boredom at bay. Back then, portable technology was scarce, so I found excitement and adventure by exploring new places, building fantastic structures with LEGOs, and weaving imaginary tales in my mind. Fast forward to today, and we find that many people, especially children, turn to digital sources to escape the clutches of boredom.

One of the most profound impacts pocketable smart devices have had on our lives is the erosion of our ability to tolerate boredom. Stuck at a red light? We instinctively reach for our phones. Waiting at the doctor's office? It's time to check our emails. Finding ourselves momentarily unoccupied at a social gathering? We resort to Facebook or YouTube for entertainment. We've replaced every idle moment with input from the web, as though we're afraid to be alone with our thoughts. I admit, I'm not immune to this behavior. My restless desire to constantly seek new information from the internet led me to implement a no-internet challenge for five days each month. Although I use a Light Phone 2 for personal communication, my Surface Go has gradually become a hindrance in my journey toward a low-tech lifestyle. I find myself constantly checking emails, responding to chat conversations, or browsing the web through its efficient and user-friendly interface.

To address this, my no-internet challenge imposes strict limitations on my access to the internet's most popular tools. By creating a software and hardware environment that denies access to email, web browsing, entertainment, and other connected resources, I've deliberately reintroduced boredom into my life. I've dubbed these "offline days" and document the significant hurdles I face while living in the 21st century without the convenience of smart tools. During these days, I encounter inconveniences like the lack of QR codes for transportation or dining, the need to print tickets for concerts and events, and the unavailability of a yellow pages booklet to find addresses and phone numbers. These minor nuisances underscore just how dependent we've become on smart devices and instant access to information. The purpose of these five offline days is to reclaim personal agency, decrease reliance on modern technology, and reacquaint myself with the lost art of boredom. I've found that the most effective way to renew our relationship with boredom is to cut off access to the source of infinite information. Embracing boredom can be a powerful catalyst for those seeking to boost productivity and unleash creativity in their lives. By intentionally creating space for boredom, we allow our minds to wander, reflect, and generate original thoughts and ideas that might otherwise be drowned out by the constant influx of digital distractions.

In her book Bored and Brilliant, Manoush Zomorodi highlights the importance of originality and how boredom helps us achieve it. She states, "Boredom is the gateway to mind-wandering, which helps our brains create those new connections that can solve anything from planning dinner to a breakthrough in combating global warming." [1] Most of us may not recall, but our original thoughts and creations emerged out of boredom. Boredom consumed our time, and we engaged with it during our formative years, ultimately deciding to take ownership of our thoughts to address the problems around us. That's why living with low-tech can benefit your work, education, or life in general. The absence of a constant flow of information from the internet's depths allows your brain the space to think, create, and tackle the issues you currently face. While there is a time for healthy distractions, constantly relying on external input to avoid our thoughts is generally unproductive. A balanced use of smart devices, combined with restraints throughout your day, can help you reset and gain perspective. In the following pages, I hope to share some ideas to engage with boredom.

Pick up the pace

One of my favorite methods for accessing new ideas and solving problems involves taking 15-minute walks. During my years at Andrew's University, where I earned my Master's Degree in Divinity, I developed an effective walking technique to write papers. Using a pomodoro timer, I would dedicate fifty minutes to writing my research papers in the library and then take a ten to fifteen-minute walk immediately afterward. Regardless of the season, I consistently allocated time for walking between research sessions to help me sort out my ideas and create a structure for my writing. This approach enabled me to produce high-quality papers in relatively short periods of time, as I maintained focus on my work while also allowing room for idea generation. My walks around the James White library provided a framework for my papers and allowed my brain the necessary time to organize and process information efficiently. I'm writing this book using the same technique: 300 words, walk the dog, cycle through, and finish after three sessions. If you're reading this sentence, it means the method still holds value to this day.

Walking provides not only mental benefits but also significant physical advantages. A September 2022 article in the New York Times highlighted new studies that analyzed data from activity trackers. Researchers discovered that walking at a brisk pace for about 30 minutes a day led to a reduced risk of heart disease, cancer, dementia, and death, compared to walking a similar number of steps but at a slower pace. This evidence emphasizes the importance of integrating brisk walking into our daily routines to improve our overall health and well-being. Interestingly, these thirty-minute brisk walking sessions do not have to occur continuously. Breaking them down into two or three 10-minute sessions throughout the day provides the same benefits as one extended 30-minute session. This flexibility allows individuals with busy schedules or those who prefer shorter bouts of activity to still reap the rewards of brisk walking. Ultimately, it's the speed at which you walk, rather than the duration, that makes the difference in promoting better health and reducing the risk of various ailments.[2]

The art of walking also helps us reclaim a part of our human potential that smart devices have increasingly diminished. As we spend more time in front of screens, our levels of physical activity have steadily decreased. A systematic review of multiple experiments regarding smartphone use and sedentary activity concluded that "those who use the smartphone less spend less time sitting than those who have a more continuous use of it." [3] With data suggesting that 31% of the world's population is not meeting the minimum recommendations for physical activity, the situation becomes increasingly concerning. [4] As technology offers us more conveniences, our interaction with the outside world lessens, and we inadvertently sacrifice our mental and physical development for the sake of "convenience."

For instance, purchasing groceries used to require time and physical effort – walking through store aisles, pushing shopping carts, and carrying bags to our cars. Now, with online grocery shopping and delivery, we pay someone else to bring our groceries to our doorstep, sparing us that effort. Another example is how technology has transformed the way we play. Growing up, I remember engaging in physical activities like soccer or hide-and-seek with my friends. As touchscreen devices and multiplayer games became more accessible, our playtime increasingly moved indoors and in front of screens. This shift in behavior intensified as I moved to the United States and experienced the proliferation of new games on the App Store.While gaming consoles like Xbox, Playstation, and Gamecube have existed for decades, the ubiquity of pocketable devices has been a major disrupting force in our physical activity levels. To counteract the negative effects of sedentary behavior, we must reintroduce low-tech play into our lives, such as sports or even playing with LEGOs. By embracing these activities, we can break the cycle of sedentary behavior and reconnect with the world around us.

Embracing the simple act of walking can unlock creativity, enhance problem-solving skills, and provide significant mental and physical benefits. By incorporating brisk walking into our daily routines, we can improve our overall health and well-being, even in the midst of our increasingly screen-centric world. In this context, boredom transforms into an ally for our minds and bodies, allowing us to reconnect with ourselves and the world around us.

Calming Your Mind

A second approach to dealing with boredom is to create space for silence and tranquility. In today's world, our minds are constantly bombarded with vast amounts of content. Some estimates suggest that our exposure to brands and passive advertising ranges between 4,000 and

10,000 messages per day. [5]While the actual number of intrusive ads is much lower at around 300, a 2018 study from the Czech Republic found that our engagement with media messaging saturates our days. The researchers examined the pervasiveness of advertisements in people's lives and discovered that even public spaces contained an average of two promotions within a 90-second span. [6] Although limited to a specific country, it's not hard to imagine how media competes for our attention with tremendous intensity making our minds process information constantly.

Two helpful methods I've employed during my periods of boredom that calm my mind are coloring and exercise. These activities offer pockets of silence throughout my day, allowing me to reflect and focus on my mind and body instead of stressing about work or other life challenges. When I step outside for a run with my dog, I concentrate on my body's signals – my breathing, heart rate, and joint movements. Tuning into these signals and appreciating the natural beauty of the parks I frequent has positively impacted my mood and concentration during high-input activities at work. It serves as a reminder that there are moments in my day when I can find solace in nature and enjoy it for what it is.

Chris Bailey, author of Calming Your Mind, encourages readers to embrace similar low-stimulus activities. In the section on boredom in his book, he details how he attempted to engage with silence and boredom in some unconventional ways over 31 days. Examples from his experience include painting a canvas with one color, reading the iTunes terms and conditions, and watching a clock tick for an hour. While these activities may seem absurd to some, Bailey's experiment provided a bridge from high to low-stimulation activities. He explains that low stimulation allows our thoughts to settle instead of constantly receiving input from external sources.[7] Incorporating these seemingly dull activities into our daily routines can reduce stress and encourage deep thinking about the information stored in our brains.

Two commonly suggested practices from researchers and other books that I have yet to integrate into my lifestyle are journaling and meditation. Although I don't have personal experience with these activities, numerous studies have highlighted the positive impact these analog practices can have on quality of life. Journaling has been linked to reducing anxiety and depression[8], enhancing immune function[9], and improving memory[10]. Neurologist Judy Wills observes, "The practice of writing can enhance the brain's intake, processing, retaining, and retrieving of information... it promotes the brain's attentive focus ... boosts long-term memory, illuminates patterns, gives the brain time for reflection, and when well-guided, is a source of conceptual development and stimulus of the brain's highest cognition."[11] Understanding the research on the benefits of expression through writing highlights the importance of prioritizing time for contemplation and emotional regulation as humans. Nowadays, smartphones bombard us with a constant stream of information, making it challenging to process everything we encounter.

Meditation is another practice that offers an array of benefits for mental well-being. Whether guided or not, meditation has positive correlations with healthy aging[12], emotional regulation[13], and managing depression or anxiety conditions[14]. Incorporating meditation into your daily routine can help you develop mindfulness and foster a sense of inner calm. By learning to focus on the present moment, you can cultivate an awareness that enables you to better manage stress and improve mental clarity. In combination with journaling, meditation can significantly improve your state of mind and help fill the void left by excessive screen time or aimless web browsing. Both practices offer opportunities to engage in meaningful self-reflection, promoting personal growth and enhancing overall well-being.

A final method to find moments of calm and develop critical thinking is by engaging in deep reading with physical books. Mary Ann Wolf, Director of the Center for Dyslexia, Diverse Learners, and Social Justice at UCLA, describes deep reading as a process where readers immerse themselves in the text, enabling reflection and critical thinking. Digital devices, however, may impede this skill development, as their design, with constant notifications and distractions, disrupts concentration and makes sustained attention challenging. Wolf states, "multitasking, constant interruption, lack of focus, and the need for speed may deter the development of the deep-reading processes that are so important to many domains of our lives."[15] Therefore, cultivating deep reading skills requires an environment free from distractions and interruptions and minimizing multitasking while reading.

Physical books offer a more conducive deep reading experience due to the tactile sensations of page-turning, the smell of ink, and the ability to underline or highlight passages. Wolf emphasizes, "The physicality of the book itself is an important aspect of deep reading, and one that we may lose if we rely exclusively on digital devices."[16] Some e-readers replicate this experience, allowing users to highlight or take notes, but they don't provide the full benefits of a physical book. Digital devices can also affect reading speed, promoting a 'flicking' behavior, as Mary Ann notes, where readers rapidly scroll through a text, scanning for specific words or phrases rather than deeply engaging with the material. To read deeply and critically, it's essential to read slowly and reflect on the content.

Deep reading encompasses not only the act of reading but also the ability to engage in reflective and analytical thinking, which forms the foundation of knowledge acquisition. To navigate the complex social, economic, and political issues of our time, we must read closely, analyze, interpret, and integrate new information with prior knowledge, and write with clarity and purpose. Cultivating deep reading skills through physical books or digital devices and creating a conducive environment for concentration, free from distractions and interruptions, allows us to develop the ability to read deeply and critically, crucial for success in today's world.

Although coloring books, exercise, and reading are my preferred methods for embracing boredom, other ways such as meditating, praying, woodworking, or taking a nap are equally valid for calming your day. Learning to live in silence and low stimulation can create new pathways in your life and lead to mindful productivity in work and personal relationships. By incorporating more analog-based activities into our lives and reducing digital input from the internet, these practices become effective tools to combat boredom and maintain stillness in our fast-paced world.

Creating Community

Another approach to mastering boredom involves engaging meaningfully with your local community. As a child, I recall eliminating idleness by visiting my friend's house, playing soccer, and conversing until dinner time. My friend Jeffry and I would spend hours discussing girls, our favorite teams, and current events. I felt a sense of sadness when leaving his house, even though I knew we would meet again the next day. Although adulthood brings work and tight schedules, we can still reconnect with our local community to recapture that youthful sense of serendipity. Local lounges or coffee shops offer opportunities to meet neighbors and organize activities that create meaningful change in our habits. This book aims to help you change your lifestyle. Making an effort to spend more time with friends, family, or coworkers not only provides momentary satisfaction but also restructures how you allocate your time. For those new to a neighborhood, websites like meetup.com can be a gateway to meeting new people and exploring experiences beyond your comfort zone. After the initial interaction, we can invite new friends to our homes and continue learning about each other's lives and creating deeper bonds.

As I transitioned from high to low technology use, my days shifted from being consumed by online information to forging connections outside my home. Whether it's playing pickleball on Mondays or attending PowerPoint parties once a month[17], limited web access encourages me to seek meaningful connections beyond work. Building a community with friends or acquaintances can lead to deeper satisfaction in daily tasks. Recent research suggests even brief interactions with strangers can positively impact our psychosocial well-being and enhance our perception of the community.[18] [19]

While talking to strangers isn't for everyone[20], I've discovered that asking about someone's day on public transportation or striking up small conversations with a barista can foster a positive atmosphere in our increasingly individualistic world. Engaging with our community shifts the way we interact and helps preserve social cohesion. Instead of scrolling through targeted ads, we can immerse ourselves in our local coffee shop, bar, or business and interact with it more meaningfully. By exploring what our town offers, we can better understand its strengths and weaknesses. However, a word of caution for those completely avoiding web-related activities: the internet and smart devices do provide a way to interact with distant loved ones. Although not perfect, video conferencing software can help maintain relationships with various social groups. Acknowledging its limitations and using it sparingly can help us strike a balance between preserving existing relationships and cultivating new local ones. Personally, I know that in-person interactions cover topics seldom discussed in video calls, but such tools can be useful for staying connected with faraway family members.

The ultimate habit to conquer boredom is learning new skills. As you free up time from previous digital activities, the natural inclination to acquire information or combat idleness will emerge. Utilizing this time to create or satisfy your curiosity is a fantastic way to be purposeful and direct your interests towards new horizons. Embracing the opportunity to learn new skills not only enriches our lives but also develops a greater sense of self-efficacy and accomplishment. This can take many forms, such as exploring a new artistic medium, picking up a musical instrument, learning a new sport, or even delving into an unfamiliar academic subject. The key is to choose activities that genuinely interest and engage you, as this will help sustain motivation and make the learning process enjoyable rather than a chore.

My YouTube channel's creation is a prime example of utilizing free time productively. During the 2020 lockdown, I found myself with more free time than I could have ever imagined. Work came to a halt, stores closed, and my local community stayed home. I believe we all experienced similar circumstances to some extent. While the initial days were extremely challenging, I saw a unique opportunity during this period. I dedicated two hours each day to learning how to shoot videos, take photos, and create content. Some of this time was, indeed, spent in front of a screen. However, I believe there's a distinction between passively staring at a screen for entertainment and actively seeking input for self-improvement. One pacifies our boredom and inputs information, while the other creates a way for us to extract information and put it into practice in the analog world.

As I connected with content creators, learned the intricacies of video editing, and read about common mistakes for those entering the digital economy, I rekindled a sense of curiosity and creativity during a difficult time. Although my YouTube channel remains intentionally a hobby, it serves as a creative outlet allowing me to share my passion for helping people reduce their internet use (ironically, I know). By addressing boredom through knowledge acquisition, we can mitigate negative feelings and pursue long-lost dreams.

Embracing Boredom

As I continue my journey to decrease reliance on high-tech products and services, new hobbies and learning outcomes have become my goals. Analog activities geared towards learning, like reading books, acquiring new skills, or practicing a new language, are my favorite ways to alleviate boredom. Similarly, I recognize that silence, coloring, meditation, journaling, and other calming activities must be part of a balanced approach to boredom. Whatever path you decide is best for you, remember that boredom unlocks new possibilities for our newfound time. It creates pockets of space where we can slow down, spark creativity and curiosity without adding stress to our lives. How we utilize this gift is entirely up to us.

1. Zomorodi, M. (2017). Bored and Brilliant: How Spacing Out Can Unlock Your Most Productive and Creative Self. St. Martin's Press.
2. Gorman, A. (2022, September 20). Fast Walking May Be Better Than Running for Health. The New York Times. https://www.nytimes.com/2022/09/20/well/move/fast-walking-exercise-intensity.html.
3. Kohl, H. W., Craig, C. L., Lambert, E. V., Inoue, S., Alkandari, J. R., Leetongin, G., ... & Lancet Physical Activity Series Working Group. (2012). The pandemic of physical inactivity: global action for public health. The Lancet, 380(9838), 294-305. https://doi.org/10.1016/S0140-6736(12)60898-8
4. Fong, S. S. M., Ng, S. S. W., & Guo, X. (2019). Effects of smartphone use on health and well-being: A systematic review and meta-analysis. Frontiers in Psychology, 10, 1307. https://doi.org/10.3389/fpsyg.2019.01307
5. Marshall, R. (2015, September 10). HOW MANY ADS DO YOU SEE IN ONE DAY? Retrieved from https://www.redcrowmarketing.com/2015/09/10/many-ads-see-one-day/

6. Tomčík, M., & Rosenlacher, P. (2018). Number of advertisements per day and their relevance to consumers. Journal of Competitiveness, 10(4), 90-106. https://doi.org/10.7441/joc.2018.04.06
7. Bailey, C. (2022). Calming Your Mind: How to Reduce Anxiety and Stress, Boost Productivity, and Increase Happiness. Macmillan.
8. Hasanzadeh, P., Fallahi Khoshknab, M., & Norozi, K. (2012). Impacts of Journaling on Anxiety and Stress in Multiple Sclerosis Patients. CMJA, 2(2), 183-193. Retrieved from http://cmja.arakmu.ac.ir/article-1-21-en.html
Stice, E., Burton, E., Bearman, S. K., & Rohde, P. (2007). Randomized trial of a brief depression prevention program: an elusive search for a psychosocial placebo control condition. Behavior research and therapy, 45(5), 863-876. doi: 10.1016/j.brat.2006.08.008. PMID: 17007812; PMCID: PMC2330269.
9. Baikie, K., & Wilhelm, K. (2005). Emotional and physical health benefits of expressive writing. Advances in Psychiatric Treatment, 11(5), 338-346. doi:10.1192/apt.11.5.338

10. Yogo, M., & Fujihara, S. (2010). Working memory capacity can be improved by expressive writing: A randomized experiment in a Japanese sample. British Journal of Health Psychology, 15(4), 663-674. doi: 10.1348/135910707X252440.

11. Willis, J. (2017, March 9). Writing and Executive Function: Brain Research Can Inform Writing Instruction. Edutopia. Retrieved from https://www.edutopia.org/blog/writing-executive-function-brain-research-judy-willis

12. Klimecki, O., Marchant, N. L., Lutz, A., Poisnel, G., Chételat, G., & Collette, F. (2019). The impact of meditation on healthy ageing — the current state of knowledge and a roadmap to future directions. Current Opinion in Psychology, 28, 223-228. https://doi.org/10.1016/j.copsyc.2019.01.006

13. Valim, C. P. R. A. T., Marques, L. M., & Boggio, P. S. (2019). A Positive Emotional-Based Meditation but Not Mindfulness-Based Meditation Improves Emotion Regulation. Frontiers in Psychology, 10, 647. https://doi.org/10.3389/fpsyg.2019.00647

14. Saeed, S. A., Cunningham, K., & Bloch, R. M. (2019). Depression and Anxiety Disorders: Benefits of Exercise, Yoga, and Meditation. American Family Physician, 99(10), 620-627.

15. Wolf, Maryanne. (2018, June 18). Cultivating Deep Reading in a Digital Age. ABC Religion and Ethics. Retrieved from https://www.abc.net.au/religion/maryanne-wolf-cultivating-deep-reading-in-a-digital-age/102001224
16. Ibid.
17. A PowerPoint party is a 2 hour or so event where people come and share their knowledge about any given topic. It's a seven minute presentation that can give you insight into what people do on their spare time. Thanks to Ivan and Olivia Ruiz-Knott for organizing these and creating connections with people.
18. Sandstrom, G. M., & Dunn, E. W. (2013). Is efficiency overrated? Minimal social interactions lead to belonging and positive affect. Social Psychological & Personality Science, 5(4), 436-441. https://doi.org/10.1177/1948550613502990
19. Sandstrom, G. M., Boothby, E. J., & Cooney, G. (2022). Talking to strangers: A week-long intervention reduces psychological barriers to social connection. Journal of Experimental Social Psychology, 102, 104356. https://doi.org/10.1016/j.jesp.2022.104356

20. Sandstrom, G. M., & Boothby, E. J. (2021). Why do people avoid talking to strangers? A mini meta-analysis of predicted fears and actual experiences talking to a stranger. Self and Identity, 20(1), 47-71. https://doi.org/10.1080/15298868.2020.1816568

Chapter 6

What will my family think?

In my journey through the dumbphone subreddit, I stumbled upon a recurring theme: users grappling with the disapproval of family and friends as they chose to adopt a basic phone. The widespread reliance on messaging apps like WhatsApp and iMessage has left those who've opted for minimalism struggling to balance social and familial expectations with their desire for simplicity. One particular story comes to mind, where a user described the disappointment of their loved ones as they made the switch, leaving them feeling isolated and torn between maintaining their newfound digital tranquility and the need to stay connected.

In this chapter, we'll delve into these challenges, weaving together the stories and experiences of those who have faced this dilemma. Along the way, we'll uncover alternative methods of staying in touch with the people who matter most, all while upholding a mindful and deliberate approach to communication. Through these narratives, we hope to offer support and encouragement to those on their own journey towards a more balanced relationship with technology.

Who are you doing this for?

When my wife and I relocated to Denver in 2022, we were faced with a crucial decision – should we purchase a second car, or continue relying on our trusty 2004 Toyota Camry? After weighing our options, I decided to take an unconventional approach and chose an electric bike for my daily commute. Despite my new workplace being roughly 10 miles away, the savings were substantial, and the prospect of experimenting with alternative modes of transportation was enticing. However, when we moved in January, right before the peak of winter, my family members were skeptical. They expressed concerns about my safety, the feasibility of this lifestyle in snowy conditions, and the overall practicality of my decision. My parents jokingly questioned the viability of this "crazy" idea, while my in-laws urged me to reconsider and opt for a more traditional vehicle.

A year after using public transportation and my electric bike, I am wholeheartedly convinced that buying another car was unnecessary. This lifestyle change has had a profoundly positive impact on my life, and I am grateful for having the courage to explore a new mode of transportation. The benefits are numerous: my family has saved a significant amount of money, I've incorporated additional exercise into my daily routine, and my job remains unaffected. Although my situation may be unique due to my flexible schedule, I am content with the positive changes that have resulted from my unconventional choice. This experience has reminded me of the time I transitioned to vegetarianism, despite my parents' disappointment during holiday visits as they could no longer serve me their delicious meals. I made the decision to change my diet for myself, with the goal of improving my health. I didn't do it for them.

It's essential to recognize that societal pressures and norms often influence our decisions, but we should challenge ourselves to explore alternative options that might be healthier or more cost-effective. The message here is that minimizing digital access to smart devices is a personal choice that can yield various benefits. It's not about pleasing others but prioritizing individual well-being when making this decision. Adopting such a shift in perspective can lead to more mindful and intentional use of technology. In the pursuit of a healthier and more conscious lifestyle, embracing unconventional choices and evaluating their impact becomes crucial. By stepping outside our comfort zones and welcoming new ideas and approaches, we can uncover untapped potential and foster positive change, all while remaining true to our values and aspirations.

It's important to note that making positive changes in your life doesn't mean alienating loved ones. Instead, it's a matter of setting boundaries and sticking to them. In my case, I've established a communication system that works for me. I call my loved ones once a week and chat only on desktop clients. To handle iMessage groups, I use email, and for WhatsApp, I use Bluestacks, an Android operating system emulator. By changing the way I communicate from my pocket to my office at home, I am able to stay focused on the present without being distracted by constant notifications. Although this means I may occasionally be late to the conversation and not always able to interact in real-time with everyone's thoughts, it's a tradeoff I'm willing to make to create boundaries and limits for my digital consumption. This system has allowed me to remain connected with important messages and discussions without having to constantly listen to pings coming from my phone's speaker.

As I've navigated these changes in my life, I've discovered that it's possible to strike a balance between embracing alternative options and maintaining connection with those who matter most. By setting boundaries and establishing effective communication systems, we can minimize our reliance on smart devices while still staying in touch with our loved ones. It's about finding the right balance that allows us to live our lives on our terms, while also nurturing the relationships that enrich our lives.

Make the most when you are present

I must confess, I have a deep affection for technology. I enjoy watching TV, consuming content, and playing video games. My inability to restrain myself is what prompted me to explore a lifestyle change and reduce my interaction with single-purpose devices. I know all too well that when something new is presented to me, I need to be mindful and establish healthy boundaries around it. During Christmas 2022, my wife and I traveled to California to spend time with both of our families. Sitting in front of the 60-inch TV in my grandma's living room, I binge-watched the fifth season of Cobra Kai on Netflix. It was right there, tempting me to waste hours watching it instead of engaging in meaningful conversations with my grandmother. Rather than showing interest in my aunt and uncle's latest news and topics of discussion, I chose to consume content from a screen. Later that evening, we went to dinner, and I managed to catch up with them, but I had failed to remain focused on what truly mattered.

In contrast, just a few days earlier, my brother-in-law, his girlfriend, my mother-in-law, and my wife spent four days working together on a Mandalorian-themed puzzle. It was a stark contrast to how I spent my time with my own family, where I wasted the only day I had to interact with them. I share this story as a reminder that my dedigitalization journey is ongoing, and it serves as a cautionary tale for others. No matter how far we have delved into a low-tech lifestyle, the allure of screens and shiny new features will be there, waiting to ensnare us once more. For those who have struggled with excessive screen use, keeping smart devices and addictive apps at bay requires a daily conscious effort.

Technology companies employ thousands of engineers to create digital technologies designed to lure us in and keep us using their services as they mine our data. Nir Eyal, author of Hooked: How to Build Habit-Forming Products, provides numerous examples of how to develop apps and services that keep users coming back for more. In his book, he states, "To change behavior, products must ensure the user feels in control. People must want to use the service, not feel they have to." As I sat in front of my grandma's TV, I was, in theory, in control. I could have turned it off, gone to the table, pulled out a board game, and initiated conversation with my family. But I didn't. Netflix exploited my interest in the Karate Kid reboot, automatically prompted me to watch the next episode, and anticipated my response. They made their money that day, as I chose the path of least resistance and spent about six hours using their streaming service.

To avoid falling into the trap of excessive screen time, we must actively seek ways to maintain our connection with family and friends while minimizing our reliance on screens. One approach is to allocate specific times for face-to-face conversations, ensuring that we are truly present and engaged during those moments. Additionally, we can participate in shared activities like board games, puzzles, or outdoor pursuits, which not only foster bonding but also offer a refreshing alternative to digital distractions. By consciously making an effort to establish a healthy balance between our digital and real-world interactions, we can cultivate meaningful relationships and create lasting memories with our loved ones.

The ultimate goal of minimizing our screen use is to become more connected with others and ourselves. We cannot claim to be mindful and present without sharing these qualities in our interactions with the people who matter most in our lives. By prioritizing quality time with our loved ones and engaging in activities that promote genuine connection, we can reap the benefits of a more balanced and fulfilling life. This shift in focus allows us to rediscover the joys of simple, shared experiences, fostering a deeper sense of understanding and appreciation for the people around us. In the end, it is through these meaningful connections that we truly enrich our lives and nurture our well-being.

Keep yourself (and your family) sane

As I embarked on my journey to minimize digital access to smart devices, I realized the importance of maintaining clear communication with my family and friends. I came across a post on the Light Phone subreddit where a user shared their clever solution. When switching from an iPhone to a minimalist device, they sent a note outlining their preferred methods of contact to their closest friends and family. It stated that if something was urgent, they could call, but otherwise, they would respond within 24-48 hours. This reassured their loved ones, who might have been alarmed by a lack of immediate response, which is often expected in today's culture.

The user's story inspired me to adopt a similar approach. They remained mindful about responding promptly to messages from those who didn't call repeatedly throughout the day. By not constantly carrying distracting technology in their pocket, they found a better balance between staying connected with loved ones and avoiding the constant distractions that come with being tethered to a smartphone. This served as an excellent reminder that clear communication is essential when it comes to managing our relationships in the digital age.

Seeing the success of their method, I decided to implement it in my life. It provided a clear set of expectations for anyone trying to reach me, demonstrating that my priorities were focused on indulging in hobbies and pursuing my desires, rather than being constantly distracted by technology. By communicating my new approach in a precise and straightforward manner, I was able to establish a sense of predictability that encouraged more frequent calls and reduced texting. My ultimate objective was to increase face-to-face interactions with others, and I was pleased to see that I successfully achieved this goal.

Of course, everyone's situation is unique, but setting expectations and boundaries with loved ones is crucial when transitioning to a low-tech lifestyle. To help others with this process, I created a simple template:

"Hi [insert name], I wanted to let you know that I'm making a conscious effort to simplify my digital life. As part of that, I'll be transitioning to a basic phone in the near future. If you need to reach me urgently, please give me a call. Otherwise, I'll be checking my texts less frequently. I hope you understand, and I look forward to catching up with you soon!"

Being upfront about my intentions and providing clear guidelines for communication helped ensure a smoother transition and avoided any misunderstandings or hurt feelings. Whether you choose to use the above note or create your own version, sending it to friends and family in advance of your switch will pave the way for a smoother transition and establish clear expectations for the future.

As I reflect on this experience, I realize that the key to success lies not only in setting boundaries and expectations, but also in finding creative ways to maintain connections with those who matter most. As we continue to explore new paths and minimize our dependence on smart devices, we learn to appreciate the genuine connections and the moments of joy that life has to offer.

The Foyer and the Ethernet Room

In our quest to prioritize our loved ones and minimize digital distractions, two healthy practices have emerged as game-changers: using a charging station in the entrance of our home and limiting internet access to one room only. The foyer method, as I like to call it, is a simple yet effective way to keep smart devices out of sight and mind while still allowing for necessary functionality. I've observed my wife, who has mastered this technique, put her phone in the charging station as soon as she arrives home from work, leaving it there until the next morning. If she needs to take a call or respond to a message in the evening, she sets her phone to loud and attends to it only when necessary. By untethering herself from the constant demands of technology, she is able to fully engage with our home and family. As for me, I am still learning to adopt this behavior. While I use a Light Phone 2, I sometimes listen to podcasts or music in the house, forgetting to put down my phone or laptop. However, I am determined to improve by not only using the foyer method but also setting time constraints on device usage and embracing a shutdown ritual. Many authors recommend such practices as they can significantly enhance overall well-being and strengthen relationships in the home.

Another step we desire in order to prioritize our loved ones and minimize distractions is to limit internet access to a wired connection only. Wi-Fi has become ubiquitous in our modern age, but those of us who grew up in the 90s or early 2000s may remember the sound of dial-up connecting our computers to the web. Despite its limitations, it provided a sense of order and predictability that allowed us to engage in other activities without being constantly interrupted by digital distractions. With the proliferation of smartphones and wireless devices, Wi-Fi has become a necessary component for their full functionality. However, by setting physical boundaries within our homes, we can maintain a healthy balance and strengthen our relationships with those around us. By designating a specific room or area for wired internet access, we can still enjoy the benefits of online connectivity while keeping it in its proper place and preserving our focus on what matters most.

Embarking on this low-tech journey, we have come to understand three important aspects of the lifestyle. First, it is important to remember that this change is for our personal benefit, and we don't need to convince others of its advantages. While setting clear expectations with loved ones can be helpful, this journey is ultimately ours to undertake. Second, recognizing the pervasive nature of digital distractions and being patient with ourselves as we work to reduce our dependency on smart devices is crucial. It's essential to prioritize meaningful interactions with family and friends, and view any challenges or setbacks as learning experiences. Finally, implementing physical limitations on our digital access can be an effective strategy for enhancing personal relationships. By using a wired internet connection, we can limit the reach of digital distractions and create space for more analog activities. This approach may take some getting used to, but it can ultimately provide significant benefits to our well-being and relationships. As a bonus, with no Wi-Fi password to worry about, we've finally escaped the never-ending question, "What's the Wi-Fi password?" once and for all.

CHAPTER 7

IS MY PROFESSION COMPATIBLE WITH LOW TECH?

In a world that seemed to shift overnight, I made the conscious decision to switch to a basic phone, not knowing how challenging this would be during the unfolding pandemic. As my job evolved from a hands-on, physical presence to an entirely digital landscape, I found myself increasingly reliant on Zoom, Google Meet, and a myriad of other online platforms to connect with volunteers and do my job. While technology provided an essential lifeline during those unprecedented times, I soon faced the stark reality of my basic phone's limitations in meeting my job's demands.

Despite the difficulties, I count myself fortunate to have retained my job throughout the pandemic, with the luxury of working remotely from home. As the months rolled by, my work gradually transitioned back to in-person events and meetings, necessitating the adoption of new software and tools. From QR codes to two-factor authentication accounts, the lockdowns of 2020 revolutionized the way we interact with one another. Admittedly, the breakneck pace of change can be overwhelming at times, but I've learned to adapt and embrace the advantages technology can offer—albeit with a newfound appreciation for its limitations.

Now, after two full years of adjusting to this novel system, there is still room for improvement in how we interact with work and the digital tools that surround it. Smart devices remain indispensable for certain tasks, but this doesn't mean we can't reduce their usage or even eliminate it altogether. In my journey, I've discovered that striking a balance between leveraging the benefits of technology and maintaining a low-tech lifestyle is an ongoing process. With mindfulness, intention, and a willingness to embrace change, we can navigate the complexities of the digital age while still preserving the core values of simplicity and human connection.

VBLCCP

As a transfer student settling into dorm life, I was eager to find a job on campus that would not only help me earn some extra cash but also fit seamlessly into my college schedule. When word reached me that the campus deli was hiring, I leaped at the opportunity. The prospect of crafting sandwiches and salads all day didn't bother me in the least, and I figured it would be an excellent way to forge connections with fellow students on campus. However, there was one glaring issue: the start time. The deli opened its doors at 6 AM, which required me to be there, apron on, by 4 AM to begin prepping the food. As a night owl, accustomed to late-night conversations with friends or marathon study sessions, the idea of waking up at such an ungodly hour filled me with dread.

The initial few weeks were nothing short of a Herculean struggle. I rolled out of bed each morning, bleary-eyed and irritable, fighting the urge to hit the snooze button. The trek to the deli seemed like an eternal journey, and I frequently found myself nodding off during my shift. Crafting sandwiches and salads wasn't precisely rocket science, but maintaining focus proved challenging when all I yearned for was the warm embrace of my bed. After three long months of battling this grueling routine, I recognized that something had to give. While I enjoyed the job itself, the hours were slowly but surely draining my life force. I made the difficult decision to resign and embarked on a search for a position better suited to my schedule. Fortunately, my quest was short-lived, as I soon landed a gig answering calls and creating graphics for a campus department. The hours were ideal for me, allowing me to indulge in a more reasonable sleep schedule while still providing ample time to work in the afternoons.

Furthermore, the new job proved to be far more engaging and stimulating than my stint at the deli. I took great pleasure in utilizing my creative skills to craft eye-catching flyers and captivating designs, and I genuinely relished the interactions I had with people over the phone. All in all, the new position emerged as an ideal match for my junior year lifestyle, striking a harmonious balance between rewarding work and the distinctive pace of college life.

VBLCCP, an acronym for Values-Based Lifestyle-Centric Career Planning, is a potent approach that assists individuals in navigating their career paths while aligning with their personal values and lifestyle objectives. Introduced by author and professor Cal Newport on his podcast, this concept has since aided numerous listeners in addressing the challenge of finding fulfillment in their professional lives. Newport underscores the significance of comprehending and prioritizing one's values and lifestyle goals when planning their career trajectory. He contends that "by identifying many different jobs that, if properly pursued, move you toward the life you desire... they can also help you direct the job you already have in directions that will provide you the most benefit."[1] This perspective encourages individuals to contemplate not only their professional ambitions but also their personal aspirations, such as achieving a healthy work-life balance, attaining financial stability, and seizing opportunities for growth and development. By incorporating these considerations into career planning, individuals can ensure they're on a path that aligns with their true passions and life goals, ultimately leading to greater satisfaction and success.

Utilizing VBLCCP, individuals can evaluate their current job or potential career paths by considering their values and lifestyle objectives. This process facilitates a deeper understanding of what is truly significant and meaningful in their lives and helps identify opportunities to align their work with those values. Additionally, it assists individuals in making more intentional career choices, such as seeking job opportunities that offer flexible schedules or align with their passions and interests. By asking pivotal questions regarding the level of control we have over our schedule, the intensity of our job, our living situation, our social life, and our desired work-life balance, we can gain profound insight into what we genuinely desire from our careers. This approach empowers us to prioritize what matters most, whether it's more time with family, a flexible schedule, or a specific income level.

Recent research has highlighted that being happy at work has a significant impact on both individual productivity and overall team performance.[2] When employees are content and fulfilled in their roles, they tend to be more motivated, engaged, and focused. This, in turn, can lead to increased productivity, as individuals are more likely to complete their tasks efficiently and effectively. Additionally, happy employees are more likely to assist their colleagues, collaborate effectively, and contribute positively to the team's overall success. The benefits of workplace happiness extend beyond the individual, creating a positive working environment that fosters creativity, innovation, and a sense of community. These findings make it crucial for us to explore and plan what is the best fit for our goals and aspirations.

In a world where work can easily permeate every aspect of our lives, VBLCCP offers a coherent framework for maintaining our personal values at the heart of our career decisions. By using our ideal lifestyle as a guide, we can make deliberate choices that are consistent with our priorities and cultivate a more fulfilling professional life. As I delved deeper into Cal Newport's work, his concept of the deep life became my compass for aligning my lifestyle with my objectives. Newport posits that certain fundamental categories in life must be fulfilled for humans to reach their potential: Constitution (body), Contemplation (mind), Community, and Craft (work). To implement this method, it is crucial to have a clear understanding of the tasks that fall into each category. For instance, constitution may involve exercise or physical activity, while contemplation may encompass meditation or reading. By being intentional with our time and selecting activities that align with our ideals, we can create a life that is not only productive but also satisfying.

Having been inspired by his work, I decided to allocate specific time frames for each of these categories in my typical day. For my work or Craft category, I dedicated 7 hours of my day, dividing it into 4 hours of online work and 3 hours of offline work. To ensure that I adhere to my allotted time for online work, I itemized every task I needed to complete and determined whether it could be done online or offline. This approach enabled me to distinctly separate the time I spent online from the time I spent offline, eliminating the guilt that arises from excessive time spent on the web. By adhering to my designated time for online work, I am confident that I have sufficient time each day to complete my tasks without neglecting other vital aspects of my life, such as my health and relationships. If I finish my work early, I consider it a victory and proceed with my shutdown ritual, which aids me in transitioning from work mode to relaxation mode.

Second Factor Authentication

It took me several long months to find a solution to the 2FA conundrum that has become increasingly prevalent in our digital lives. It seems like we are constantly being asked for an app-based code for almost every login we encounter. Checking your email from a new location? Tap this number on your phone's mail app. Need to speak with customer service at the bank? An SMS and email code will be sent your way. Eager to sign up for a groundbreaking service that revolutionizes the way you work? We'll send you a link to download the app to set it up. As irritating as this constant need for verification has become, I recognize the necessity of second factor authentication. It combines something you know, your password, with something you have, your phone. However, as digital services continue to multiply in the office, we now have alternatives to the app-based code plague.

One such alternative is Yubikey, a physical key that serves as a second factor authenticator. Yubikey connects to a token provided by your IT department, effectively eliminating the need to receive a code via app or SMS. While not universally available, Yubikey boasts compatibility with numerous services and products requiring authentication, including Google, Microsoft, and Dropbox. Moreover, it can be utilized to securely log in to password managers such as Bitwarden or 1Password. Yubikey offers several advantages over SMS or app-based codes. First and foremost, it is more secure. SMS messages are susceptible to interception or spoofing, leaving your accounts vulnerable to attack. Similarly, your phone could be accessed by those who manage to spoof your biometrics. Yubikey, in contrast, employs public key cryptography to provide a secure authentication method that cannot be easily hacked. Second, it is both faster and more convenient. With SMS or app codes, you must wait for the code to arrive, input it, and then wait for the website or application to confirm it. Yubikey streamlines this process, enabling quick and easy authentication. Simply connect it to the terminal, wait a few seconds, and sign in to your account. Finally, Yubikey reduces dependence on smart devices. You no longer need a smartphone or another connected device to receive codes, thereby minimizing reliance on these devices and the potential distractions they generate. If your IT department has not yet implemented a token-based service, I strongly recommend that you request they do so. This will create fewer dependencies on smart devices and minimize risks simultaneously.

From a personal standpoint, using a Yubikey has been a liberating experience for me. It permits me to use my Light phone and carry the physical key to access the software I need for work without resorting to an app on my phone. As a last resort, you can ask your IT department to provide a 2FA device and make accommodations for the lack of a smartphone. In this way, Yubikey has allowed me to maintain my preference for a basic phone while still meeting the demands of my digitally connected work environment, striking a balance between convenience and minimalism.

Mindful Mail

Email has become an inextricable part of our work lives, serving as a convenient tool for communication, organization, and information sharing with colleagues. However, this indispensable technology can also come to dominate our daily routines, diminishing our productivity and hindering our ability to cultivate relationships and renew our minds. It is crucial to understand that email doesn't have to be a 24/7 obligation; we can regain control of our lives by curbing our email consumption. I, too, have fallen prey to destructive email habits such as incessantly checking my inbox, sending poorly crafted emails, and overusing the "reply all" function. However, I have since uncovered effective strategies to minimize my email interactions and mitigate their impact on my life, enabling me to establish a healthier work-life balance and prioritize other essential aspects of my life.

One approach I've adopted to combat my destructive email habits is setting specific email hours, which I include in my email signature to inform others of the expected response times. This restricted timeframe enables me to concentrate on other critical tasks since I only check and respond to emails twice a day—once in the morning and once before my designated shutdown period. By transparently communicating these expectations, I can prioritize my time and alleviate the pressure to provide immediate responses. This strategy liberates my mind from the constant pull of email, allowing me to devote my attention to more productive and meaningful pursuits. Notably, this strategy is supported by research. Gupta et al. found that replying to emails two to four times a day can improve productivity, which in turn may lower stress[3]. Furthermore, Akbar et al. demonstrated through thermal imaging that responding to emails in a batched manner reduces the amount of time it takes to reply while simultaneously decreasing the number of frustration words used in such emails[4]. Implementing this evidence-based approach has contributed significantly to enhancing my overall efficiency and well-being.

Another tactic I've implemented to streamline my email communication is to be exceptionally clear about my expectations and requests. Whenever I send an email, I ensure it contains five key points that need to be addressed before any further correspondence: the deadline, the recipient of the product or service, a response timeline for any questions that may arise, the person to whom I will report when the task is completed, and the level of autonomy I possess in developing the product or service. By addressing all of these points in one email, I reduce the number of back-and-forth interactions and minimize frustration for everyone involved. Although crafting a clear and concise email may require a few extra minutes, it ultimately saves time and energy in the long run.

Lastly, I have made a conscious effort to prioritize phone or face-to-face interactions as my primary means of communication at work. We are all aware of the limitations of email when it comes to conveying tone, nuance, and depth of understanding. Misunderstandings can easily arise from email communication, which is why I have committed to engaging in phone or in-person conversations whenever feasible. I initiate this process by sending an email outlining my questions, concerns, and proposed steps to resolve the issue at hand. After scheduling a mutually convenient time, I call or meet with my colleague, direct report, or volunteer to discuss the matter in depth. By prioritizing direct communication, I save time that would have been spent deciphering email content, interpreting tone, and grasping the underlying message. Using calls and face-to-face interactions as a means of communication allows me to ask more profound questions, delve into the subject matter, and address most inquiries during the conversation. This approach fosters a collaborative atmosphere, signaling my desire to be a team player who resolves issues or develops products with input, creativity, and clear communication. It is a far more efficient way of working, as it minimizes the back-and-forth nature of email communication and promotes a cooperative approach to problem-solving.

Working Online

The journey to becoming a content creator on YouTube specializing in digital minimalism was not without its challenges and ironies. In 2020, I embarked on the mission of promoting digital minimalism through my videos, knowing full well that I was using an online platform to convey my message. My ultimate goal, however, was to empower my audience to embrace a life with fewer digital distractions and unnecessary apps, even if it meant losing viewers in the process. The interesting paradox was that, as I became more invested in creating and editing digital content, I remained a firm believer in the principles of digital minimalism. Digital minimalism, as defined by Cal Newport in his book of the same title, is a philosophy that encourages us to carefully evaluate the digital communication tools we use and the behaviors surrounding them, to identify those that truly add value to our lives. By intentionally eliminating low-value digital noise and optimizing our use of meaningful tools, we can significantly improve our lives.[5]

In today's increasingly digital world, many of us rely on a mix of online and offline activities to perform our jobs, making us hybrid workers. It is all too easy to feel overwhelmed or defeated by the omnipresence of technology in our lives, but it's crucial to remember that we have the power to choose how we interact with it. By taking a step back and assessing our work tasks, determining which can be done offline versus online, we can begin to clear a path towards digital minimalism. This approach does not require us to spend all of our time offline; rather, it encourages us to be deliberate about our online activities and prioritize those that genuinely add value to our lives. In the summer of 2021, my dedication to promoting digital minimalism was tested by a bout of impostor syndrome. I grappled with the seeming contradiction of advocating for minimalism while actively participating in the online world. These doubts led me to reevaluate my priorities and consider whether I should continue my YouTube channel. After much reflection, I embraced the mindset of "Be online when you must, embrace offline elsewhere." This philosophy allowed me to continue sharing valuable tips and knowledge with my audience while maintaining a balanced life. I no longer felt guilty about being online when necessary and could savor my offline time without the fear of missing out.

In conclusion, the journey to digital minimalism may be fraught with challenges and contradictions, but it is ultimately a path to a more balanced and fulfilling life. By intentionally evaluating our digital habits, focusing on the tools and behaviors that add value to our lives, and embracing a purposeful mindset, we can achieve a greater sense of control, well-being, and enjoyment in both our online and offline worlds.

1. Newport, C. (2019, May 23). The most important piece of career advice you probably never heard. Retrieved from https://calnewport.com/the-most-important-piece-of-career-advice-you-probably-never-heard-2/

2. De Clercq, D., Ul Haq, I., & Azeem, M. U. (2019). Why happy employees help: How meaningfulness, collectivism, and support transform job satisfaction into helping behaviours. Personnel Review, 49(2), 442-458. doi: 10.1108/pr-03-2018-0097

3. Gupta, A., Sharda, R. & Greve, R.A. (2011). You've got email! Does it really matter to process emails now or later?. Information Systems Frontiers, 13(5), 637-653. https://doi.org/10.1007/s10796-010-9242-4

4. Akbar, F., Bayraktaroglu, A. E., Buddharaju, P., Da, D. R., Silva, C., Gao, G., Grover, T., Gutierrez-Osuna, R., Jones, N., Mark, G., Pavlidis, I., Storer, K., Wang, Z., Wesley, A., & Zaman, S. (2019). Email makes you sweat: Examining email interruptions and stress with thermal imaging. Proceedings of the 2019 CHI Conference on Human Factors in Computing Systems, 686. doi:10.1145/3290605.3300898.

5. Cal Newport. (2019). Digital Minimalism: Choosing a Focused Life in a Noisy World. New York: Portfolio/Penguin.

Chapter 8

Being a Good Example

When I take my faithful furry friend, Luca, to the local doggy daycare, I gently remind him to "be a good example." My wife and I have invested countless hours in training our German Shorthaired Pointer, nurturing a sense of obedience and discipline within him. However, once he enters the playground and encounters new four-legged playmates, all that hard-earned progress seems to vanish. For the following hours, he indulges in sniffing, barking, and nudging with untamed enthusiasm, seemingly forgetting our expectations. Despite our inability to control his every action, we hope that he will demonstrate the lessons we've taught him to the best of his ability.

Similarly, as children, we are molded by the values instilled in us by our parents. They guide us to carry ourselves with dignity and grace, to personify the finest aspects of humanity in every situation. Nonetheless, once we step out from under their watchful eye, we must rely on our own judgment. At times, we excel in upholding their teachings, while at other moments, we stumble. Although I am not a parent myself, I have had the honor of conversing with digital minimalist parents who endeavor to lead by example. They offer invaluable insights and advice that can benefit us all. In the upcoming pages, I will delve into their stories, their challenges, and their victories, along with practical tips and quotes illustrating their journey. While all names from the parent stories have been altered to protect their privacy, their lessons hold universal significance. Let us all strive to be our best selves for the sake of those we cherish and the world we inhabit.

From Software to Satiety

Jason Crew, a software engineer from Colorado and father of four, found himself grappling with digital burnout in January 2021 after years of continuously working in front of screens. Although he used his phone to capture precious moments with his children, stay connected with family, and engage with social media, he couldn't shake the feeling that screens had become an outsized part of his parenting. "One of the biggest mistakes I made during the pandemic was buying an iPad," he admitted. "It became a crutch when I didn't feel like being present or when one of my younger ones became difficult to handle. I kept using the screen as a pacifier, rather than introducing proper ways to deal with boredom and their high energy levels."

Growing up, Jason had fond memories of playing catch with his dad, creating scrap albums, and watching photos develop in his father's darkroom studio. "It taught me patience, curiosity, and precision," he recalled. "It helped me become very careful when writing code and trying to get it right the first time." Inspired by these cherished memories, Jason resolved to reintroduce more analog activities into his family's daily life. He purchased a film camera, set up a darkroom in their home, and acquired puzzles for his younger children. Over the next two years, Jason noticed a significant improvement in his connection with his children as they bonded over these analog pastimes. As his children prepared for high school, he felt ready to introduce appropriate levels of digital learning experiences. "I know that working in the tech industry has changed my life for the better and allowed me luxuries that my parents only dreamed of," he said. "I can't say I don't want my kids to have the same lifestyle, but I do want them to realize that there are times for online work and offline activities. Maintaining a balance and having a ritual for shutting down is what I hope they gained from this time in my life."

Witnessing the positive impact of Jason's decision on his family has brought me a sense of reassurance. In an era where screens increasingly dominate children's lives, his commitment to reintroducing analog activities demonstrates that establishing meaningful connections with loved ones in a natural and engaging way is possible, even if it demands effort.

As lockdowns and remote work continue to challenge us, I can only imagine the immense pressure on parents caring for young children at home. In my own work with children and youth, their seemingly limitless energy can be exhausting. Parents who handle this daily without compensation, while also planning for their children's futures across multiple domains, certainly deserve our utmost respect and admiration. Looking back on my own childhood, I now appreciate why my parents encouraged me to play outside with friends and participate in physical activities like soccer. Not only did it provide a fun outlet for excess energy, but it also helped me be calmer and more relaxed when I returned home. Parenting is undeniably a challenging and demanding job, and I am grateful to see that Jason is setting a positive example for his children by prioritizing quality time and meaningful activities. Although he cannot control every aspect of his children's lives, he is doing his best to create a nurturing and supportive environment that will help them flourish.

Handling a small business with balance

In 2014, Nancy Johnson discovered her passion for crafting handbags, a hobby that quickly gained traction in 2016 thanks to Etsy, an e-commerce platform for creators. Nancy's handbag-making online business not only enables her family to spend more quality time together but also allows them to enjoy vacations across the United States and Europe. "Working online has been one of the biggest blessings for my family," Nancy shared. "Since the business took off, we've been able to work in sprints and set aside time for travel every summer. During our busy season, typically in the fall, we spend about six hours per day handling customer orders, deliveries, and managing our online presence. After these demanding periods, we make a conscious effort to disconnect, bringing little to no technology with us on our trips."

Nancy's teenage daughter Emma, a junior in high school, manages the social media pages, marketing, and distribution for the business, with one important condition. "Her primary responsibility is to create graphics and publish content online," Nancy explained. "To teach her the proper use of online tools, we've set a daily time budget for her. After four hours of online customer interactions, she must take a break, and we all go for a walk outside. This routine helps us reset and teaches Emma that while online engagement is essential for the business and her skill development, it's not the only thing that matters in life."

Since 2017, Nancy and her husband have been tracking their screen time goals each week. "We jot them down on a whiteboard next to the refrigerator and update our progress throughout the week with a handy graph," Nancy divulged. "If anyone in the family is close to exceeding or surpasses their budget, it triggers an accountability meeting." Nancy elaborated, "The accountability meeting takes place only if someone hasn't communicated in advance that they'll exceed their screen time budget. It's our way of staying connected as a family and fostering meaningful interactions at the dinner table. By keeping the graph visible to everyone, we encourage each other to reduce screen usage and reserve smartphones and tablets for what matters most."

During our conversation, Nancy admitted that she often requires accountability meetings herself, as managing her online business, learning new skills through online courses, and attending to customer emails frequently keep her tethered to screens more than others. Regardless, she remains committed to engaging with her daughter when she returns from school. As I listened to Nancy's story, I realized that involving our loved ones in our goals can significantly improve our chances of achieving them. Although tech companies may portray screen time as a personal issue, living through our devices rather than with them can impact not only our well-being but also our relationships with those closest to us.

Reflecting on the Johnson family's approach to setting collective goals and holding each other accountable, it's evident that these practices can promote collaboration and meaning within the family unit. Long gone are the days of coming home and mindlessly zoning out on the couch. Instead, families can prioritize sharing their daily experiences and progress, whether it be in their social lives, careers, or digital habits. By integrating accountability into their interactions, families can harness personal connections as a means of embracing digital minimalism and fostering stronger relationships.

Screentime for family's sake

Abner had always been a dedicated worker. His job at a successful international finance firm had provided him and his family with a comfortable lifestyle. However, it came at a cost: Abner spent most of his days at the office, leaving little time for his wife, Clara, and their son, Patrick. Clara worked part-time at a local art chain in the afternoons, while Patrick attended after-school programs and daycare facilities. But as Patrick entered middle school, things began to change. He struggled academically and exhibited behavioral issues, causing concern for Abner and Clara. They knew they had to take action to help their son succeed. "The fact that the teachers at school said he was not motivated and sad all the time was the factor that made me consider taking the pay cut," Abner shared. "It wasn't easy at first because the difference in pay was going to change the way we were used to living. No more fancy vacations, shiny new tech, or anything like that."

Surprisingly, Abner's transition to a remote job did not involve a reduction in screen time, as one might expect. In fact, it meant an increase in screen usage and reliance on smart devices. His decision to make the switch was driven by his desire to be present for Patrick, who was struggling in school and displaying behavioral issues. Abner's dedication to his family is evident when he says, "I could have definitely offloaded the task to a tutor or buy my way out of the problem, but I didn't feel like that would yield the best result." Abner recognized the importance of being there for Patrick and was willing to make financial sacrifices to achieve that. He reduced Patrick's time in daycare and dedicated those hours to helping him with his academic and interpersonal development. Abner's decision to prioritize his family's well-being over financial gain is commendable and speaks to his character as a loving and committed parent.

Abner and Clara's story of prioritizing their family over financial comfort serves as a perfect example of how clarity of purpose can lead to successful problem-solving. Abner's previous job involved a long commute and little screen time, but he recognized that addressing Patrick's academic struggles required a different approach. Instead of relying on a tutor, he chose to take a pay cut and switch to a remote job that allowed him to spend more time with his family, including helping Patrick with homework and providing more support at home. Abner understood that his son's success was a top priority, and he was willing to make sacrifices to ensure that he could play an active role in his son's life.

Moreover, Abner's use of technology was not a hindrance, but rather a tool for success. He recognized that it could be used for more than just entertainment or work, and that it could help him connect with his family and provide the support they needed. Abner's willingness to adapt and utilize technology in this way is a valuable lesson for parents who may feel overwhelmed by the constant presence of screens in their lives. In the end, their example serves as a reminder that our priorities can guide us to make tough decisions and sacrifices in order to achieve success for our families. By staying focused on what matters most, we can find clarity and purpose in our lives and leverage technology as a tool to help us along the way.

Peer to Peer Leadership

As we conclude this chapter, I want to highlight a powerful example of young people challenging the norm of pervasive technology in their lives. Logan Lane, a teenager from New York, recognized the detrimental effects of constant phone use during the pandemic and decided to make a change that improved her wellbeing. In an interview with the New York Times, she described the physical and emotional toll of endlessly comparing herself to others on social media.[1] During the pandemic, her screen use skyrocketed due to school and communication being heavily reliant on smart devices.

"So physically, I could not sleep. My sleep schedule was terrible. It was not regulated, and I would stay up late most nights," Logan explained. "I also developed this indent on my fingers, where I would be holding my phone because I was just so frequently scrolling with my hands in a particular position that my fingers started shifting. And I think the rest of it's pretty — it's all more emotional than physical. But to go into that, I was just blatantly unsatisfied with myself. I was constantly seeing something better that I could be, someone prettier, someone more artistic, and I developed this level of shame about who I wasn't."

Logan's experience highlights the physical and emotional consequences that can stem from excessive technology use. Her disrupted sleep schedule and the indent on her fingers are clear indicators of the physical toll that constant screen time can have on our bodies. Sleep is crucial for our well-being, and a lack of quality sleep can negatively impact our mental and emotional health. Additionally, the physical changes she experienced in her fingers reveal how deeply ingrained technology use can become in our daily routines. On an emotional level, Logan's dissatisfaction with herself and her feelings of shame are a stark reminder of the negative impact that constant exposure to social media can have on our self-image and self-esteem. Social media often presents an idealized version of people's lives, leading us to make unhealthy comparisons and feel inadequate in various aspects of our lives. This can cause a great deal of emotional distress and contribute to a sense of worthlessness, as Logan experienced.

Determined to combat this, Logan purchased a flip phone, deleted her social media accounts, and started connecting with her peers in person. Her experience led her to start the Luddite Club at her high school in 2021. The club's origin story began when she met someone at a punk show who shared her desire to disconnect from technology. They decided to start a club that met every Sunday and engaged in activities that did not involve screens.

"We ended up going to this after-party together and really bonded. She was a freshman, but she was so well-read. And I almost saw she was who I could have been in an alternate universe freshman year if I hadn't been on my phone and hadn't been on social media," Logan recalled. "And it just came over us that we wanted to start some sort of club where we could do just what we had done that day."

Logan's mother suggested the name Luddite Club, which means a person who rejects technology. The club quickly grew as other teenagers who felt the same way about screens joined, providing a sense of community and allowing them to live a lifestyle that was not centered around technology. The story of Logan Lane and the Luddite Club is a powerful testament to how teenagers are pushing back against the norm of constant technology use in their lives. By recognizing the negative effects of being constantly connected to screens, Logan took steps to change her lifestyle and found a sense of community in doing so. Through the Luddite Club, she connected with peers who shared her values and sought to live a more intentional, screen-free lifestyle.

This story underscores the importance of stepping back from technology and being mindful of our usage. As we navigate an increasingly digital world, it is vital to be intentional about our relationship with technology and recognize when it is causing harm. By fostering connections in real life and pursuing activities that do not revolve around screens, we can find a sense of balance and fulfillment often lacking in our technology-saturated lives.

Setting up the best example

In the depths of adolescence, the world as I knew it came crashing down when my parents went through a divorce. Too young to grasp the complexities of marriage, I witnessed their struggles with the naivety of youth. But now, as a grown man and husband, I find myself unwittingly replicating some of their behaviors. When faced with tough conversations, I flee like my father once did, leaving my wife alone with her worries. Like my mother, I deflect blame and shut down emotionally in the face of conflict.

And, as my parents did, I indulge in retail therapy to chase away my sadness. I have learned from both their virtues and vices, molding myself after their example.

Despite the challenges they faced, my parents also gifted me with valuable life lessons. My mother's steadfast devotion to her loved ones taught me the rewards of selflessness. My father's tireless work ethic and unshakeable self-belief were instilled in me during our predawn trips to the farm. And, each Sunday, their dedication to volunteering and community service inspired me to make a difference in the world. Imperfect though they were, my parents provided a direct roadmap for how to navigate life's challenges and leave a positive mark upon the world. It is now up to me to follow that example and make them proud.

As a parent, it's important to remember that you cannot control every aspect of your child's life. But what you can control is the example you set for them. Your behavior, habits, and choices can have a profound impact on how your child sees the world and navigates through it. As we explore the new frontiers of the digital age, it is more crucial than ever to model healthy and balanced screen use for our children. We can teach them to use technology as a tool for learning and connecting with others, rather than as a substitute for face-to-face interaction. We can also show them the value of unplugging and spending time outdoors or engaging in other offline activities.

Ultimately, the choices we make as role models can have a ripple effect on the future of our society. By setting a positive example and teaching our children to be responsible digital citizens, we can help create a world where technology is used for good and human connection is valued above all else. Otherwise, they'll learn whatever the algorithm teaches them from the iPad in their hands. The lessons we impart and the examples we set are the legacy we leave behind, shaping the next generation and the world they will create.

---

1. Times Opinion. (Host). (2023, February 2). First Person: The Teenager Leading the Smartphone Liberation Movement. In The New York Times. Retrieved from https://www.nytimes.com/2023/02/02/opinion/teen-luddite-smartphones.html?

CHAPTER 9

MY LOW TECH LIFESTYLE

In the penultimate chapter of this book, we will delve into the many facets of my personal low-tech lifestyle, highlighting the aspects that have become increasingly important and cherished in my day-to-day life. As we navigate an ever-evolving digital landscape, the desire to strike a balance between technology and a simpler, more grounded existence has taken on greater significance. I hope the devices and concepts I share can elucidate how I am approaching the principles I have talked about in previous segments of the book.

E-Ink vs LCD

During my first year of college, I faced a significant obstacle that threatened to derail my academic pursuits – my vision began to falter. This realization struck me hard during a College Algebra class when I struggled to discern numbers and equations on the board from the back of the classroom. Alarmed, I consulted an optometrist, who informed me that excessive screen use had caused a decline in my depth perception and ability to recognize distant objects. Initially, I was in denial about the severity of my condition, trying various home remedies, such as direct sunlight exposure and homeopathic cures, which offered temporary relief but failed to provide a long-term solution. In desperation, I even abstained from screens for two weeks, hoping to improve my vision. Despite my efforts, my visual acuity continued to decline, leaving me with no choice but to accept corrective eyewear. Though the prospect of wearing lenses was initially unwelcome, I soon recognized the importance of prioritizing my ocular health.

As I grappled with my vision problems, I became increasingly aware of the perils associated with excessive screen use. I sought a solution that would allow me to engage with digital content without causing further damage to my eyesight. That's when I discovered E-ink technology, a more eye-friendly alternative that simulates the appearance of ink on paper. Unlike traditional LCD screens, E-ink devices do not emit blue light or cause eye strain, making them ideal for those who spend significant time in front of screens.

Initially, I made the transition from my iPad to an e-reader with an E-ink display, a change that had an immediate impact on my reading experience. The absence of constant notifications allowed me to focus more on my reading, whether through a physical medium or the e-reader. Admittedly, the lack of "responsiveness" was a turn-off in the beginning. However, as time passed, I adapted to the new pace of reading and came to appreciate the benefits that E-ink provided. As I searched for a more sustainable solution for my daily communication needs, I discovered the Light Phone 2. Its E-ink screen and minimalist features complemented the slower pace fostered by the e-reader experience, enabling me to manage the flow of my day more effectively. Nowadays, I barely glance at the phone and reach for it far less frequently than when I had a smartphone. The limited features and new pace have been a tremendous help in reshaping my relationship with technology and allowing me to be more present in my daily life.

The primary motivation for adopting a "slower" technology was not solely for health reasons but also to embrace a more measured approach to digital interactions. With LCD screens, information is available at a rapid pace, whereas with E-ink, users learn to be patient and appreciate the screen's refresh rate. As I continue on my journey, I am exploring the possibility of replacing my computing needs with E-ink devices. The Onyx Boox Mira Pro and Lenovo Twist are the next two devices on my radar to determine whether they can meet my productivity needs. Using E-ink for tasks like emailing and browsing websites is expected to encourage a slower workflow, allowing me to be more mindful of my digital interactions. While adopting a mindset of slowness is crucial, when it comes to screens, prioritizing eye health and embracing a new pace has proven to be a successful way for me to engage with digital technology in a more humane and balanced manner.

Operating Systems: Ya Basic

In today's increasingly connected world, distractions are everywhere. From smartphones to laptops, our devices constantly vie for our attention, making it difficult to focus on what truly matters. In pursuit of a more mindful and productive environment, I have made a conscious decision to simplify the operating systems on all my gadgets. For my laptop, I transitioned to a custom Linux system by installing a version of Ubuntu and paring it down to just ten essential apps, including indispensable work-based tools for my profession. Additionally, I've incorporated a podcast app and a reading aggregator for relaxation during breaks. By minimizing the number of apps and eliminating superfluous distractions, I have been able to enhance my focus and boost my productivity. Regarding mobile devices, I chose the Light Phone 2 and the Sunbeam F1 for my personal and work needs. Both devices offer only what is necessary, steering clear of excessive features and distractions. Optional tools such as maps and calendars assist me in staying organized and on schedule without diverting my attention from essential tasks. Podcasts and music provide entertainment when I need to escape from the world and alleviate stress. This minimalist approach has proven instrumental in helping me remain more present and engaged in my daily life.

Tough I value the convenience and accessibility of my digital devices, I have learned to appreciate the importance of disconnecting and delving into a good book. In fact, reading has become an integral part of my daily routine, offering a much-needed refuge from the relentless stimulation of the digital realm. Whenever I venture out, I ensure that I have a book with me, as it serves as an engaging alternative to combat boredom and remain connected to the world around me. During breaks or while waiting in line, I can immerse myself in another world, granting my brain a well-deserved respite from the unending stream of notifications and emails. Reading offers more than just a means to relax; it also stimulates my mind and cultivates creativity. By exposing myself to diverse ideas and viewpoints, I can broaden my perspective and generate innovative concepts. Additionally, research has shown that reading improves cognitive function and memory, making it a powerful asset for both personal and professional growth.

While I have made a conscious effort to streamline my digital devices and limit my exposure to distractions, I still recognize the value of having a more powerful operating system at my disposal. That's where my Surface Go 3 comes into play. As the most advanced OS in my arsenal, my Surface Go 3 serves as an invaluable tool for travel and other situations that demand a more connected device. Whether I need to access a specific app or work on a project that requires additional processing power, my Surface Go 3 provides me with the flexibility and versatility needed to accomplish the task. The Surface Go 3 is also equipped with LTE connectivity, which adds a layer of convenience to my digital experience. This feature allows me to stay connected on the go, enabling me to install apps, scan documents, QR codes, and perform various other tasks without needing to rely on Wi-Fi or mobile devices with Android or iOS. The LTE connection ensures that I can remain productive and access essential tools even when I'm away from a reliable internet source.

Despite its many capabilities, the Surface Go 3 is intentionally underpowered for demanding tasks such as gaming. This limitation works in my favor, as it discourages me from getting distracted by resource-intensive games that could hamper my productivity. By using a device that excels at essential tasks but falls short for more entertainment-focused activities, I can further limit my exposure to digital distractions and maintain a balanced, focused approach to my work and personal life. In conclusion, my approach to technology centers around balance and intentionality. While I acknowledge the benefits of versatile devices like the Surface Go 3, I also understand the significance of limiting my exposure to digital distractions. In today's fast-paced world, it is all too easy to become overwhelmed by the constant barrage of digital stimuli. Nevertheless, by simplifying my devices and focusing on what is truly essential, I have cultivated an environment that promotes mindfulness and intentionality. Adopting a more deliberate approach to my technology use has enabled me to become more productive, present, and fulfilled in various aspects of my life.

Television: A Conscious Decision to Disconnect

In a world where distractions are inescapable, I made a conscious decision to eliminate one of the most significant culprits - the television. In 2013, I said goodbye to my TV and have never looked back. For me, it posed too great a distraction, and I refused to allow it to become my default activity, even back when I owned a smartphone. However, the absence of a TV doesn't equate to a lack of entertainment. My spouse and I carefully select a movie to watch once a week, or occasionally, we indulge in an extended session to catch up on the latest streaming platform productions. More often than not, we download or purchase the movie and play it on a projector, enabling us to enjoy it on a big screen. Once the movie ends, we stow away the projector, ensuring it doesn't become a constant presence in our living space, enticing us to use it for other purposes.

This mindful approach to entertainment has proven immensely beneficial for both of us. By fully immersing ourselves in the movie without the interference of other content or notifications, we can genuinely appreciate the experience. Additionally, since we only watch one movie per week, we become more intentional in our selection, often engaging in thoughtful discussions to choose the perfect film. By eliminating the TV from our lives, we have managed to create an environment that fosters mindfulness and intentionality. The absence of the constant background noise produced by a television enables us to engage more deeply in other activities such as reading, cooking, or spending time outdoors. This shift in focus has allowed us to cultivate a more balanced and fulfilling lifestyle, where our attention is directed towards meaningful experiences and interactions.

Embracing Gaming, but Limiting it to the Office

The concept of gaming in the office might raise eyebrows, often leading to confusion or surprise. However, for me, this deliberate choice has significantly enhanced both my work productivity and overall well-being. As a remote worker, I spend considerable time working from home or in coffee shops. This flexibility allows me to work from almost anywhere, but it also means that my work and personal spaces can easily merge. To counter this, I designated my office as a gaming room, creating a clear separation between work and play. Entering my office signals relaxation and enjoyment, rather than work-related stress. This distinction helps me resist gaming when I should be working, and vice versa.

This arrangement doesn't mean I neglect my work responsibilities. In fact, I complete most of my productive work on the go or in coffee shops. Having a designated gaming space enables me to fully immerse myself in the latest AAA games without guilt or distractions. Moreover, gaming at the office offers benefits beyond separating work and play—it serves as a means to de-stress and unwind after a long workweek. By allocating specific time each week for gaming, I can fully embrace my passion without sacrificing work productivity or personal relationships. Intentionally incorporating gaming into one's routine can be a positive distraction when done mindfully. Planned gaming sessions offer a mental break from the demands of work and everyday life, providing an opportunity to recharge and rejuvenate. Engaging in gaming as a structured activity allows individuals to immerse themselves in an alternate world, fostering creativity, problem-solving skills, and even social connections through online communities. When gaming is scheduled and approached with intention, it becomes a valuable means of relaxation rather than an uncontrolled distraction. In this way, gaming serves as a healthy outlet for stress relief, contributing to an overall balanced and fulfilling lifestyle.

While gaming at the office or a designated location might seem unconventional, it can actually contribute to a healthier balance between work and leisure. By creating a separate space for gaming, individuals can establish clear boundaries between their work and personal lives, ensuring that distractions do not seep into their professional endeavors. This separation helps maintain focus and productivity in both domains, ultimately allowing for a more fulfilling and intentional engagement with both work and leisure activities. As long as gaming sessions are planned and approached with mindfulness, this strategy can serve as an effective way to minimize distractions, enhance overall well-being, and nurture a more balanced lifestyle.

A Day in My Life: Balancing Work, Play, and Mindfulness

As a final illustration to my low-tech lifestyle, I would like to share with you a typical day in my life. In the quiet hours of the morning, my day begins. I rise at 6:30 AM, greeted by the gentle stirrings of the world and my ever-enthusiastic dog, Luca. As dawn breaks, we embark on our invigorating 30-minute run. This isn't just exercise - it's an opportunity for me to connect with nature, to allow my thoughts to wander, and often, to absorb a podcast episode that broadens my perspective on world events or intriguing subjects. There are occasions, though, when I choose the symphony of the awakening day over digital audio, just to allow my mind the luxury of introspection. This peaceful beginning sets the tone for the day, priming my senses for the challenges and opportunities that lie ahead.

Post-run, my kitchen comes alive as I explore new breakfast recipes. This isn't a chore, but rather a creative exercise, a sensory exploration filled with tantalizing aromas and flavors. The process, far from being a mundane routine, offers me a sense of accomplishment and injects a dose of enthusiasm into the start of my day. By the time breakfast is served, I've already had a significant screen-free time, providing a digital detox that primes me for the more technologically-involved tasks ahead. With breakfast over, I plunge into the morning's work. The first part of my workday, typically lasting three hours, is an immersive session focused on offline tasks. This methodical approach allows me to tackle work without the distractions of the digital world. It's a time dedicated to networking calls, brainstorming for upcoming projects, and maintaining important relationships with clients, volunteers, and community partners. Once the offline tasks are done, I transition into my online work, carrying forward the momentum of productivity. To prevent email overload, I've instituted a practice of two 35-minute email sessions, focusing on priority emails first and quick responses next. This keeps my digital communication efficient and prevents it from dominating my workday.

After this focused work session, it's time for a well-deserved break and a second stroll around the neighborhood, a welcome interlude that recharges my senses and tires Luca out a bit more. The latter part of my workday, usually between 1 PM to 5 PM, sees me either at my office or a nearby coffee shop, finalizing work, attending meetings, and responding to pending emails. This change of location fuels my creativity and provides fresh perspectives for my projects. During my commute on my e-bike, I optimize the time by tuning into my favorite podcasts, absorbing the latest news and insights as I pedal through the streets. This dual benefit of exercise and learning leaves me invigorated and well-informed, ready to tackle the remainder of the day. As the workday winds down, I look forward to a quiet evening with my wife, a sumptuous dinner, and the immersive world of a good book. Occasionally, we indulge in a movie or catch a sports game, adding variety to our leisure activities.

In summary, my low-tech lifestyle, while unconventional, is a conscious choice that has greatly enhanced my productivity, well-being, and overall contentment. It's a harmonious blend of work, leisure, and self-care, where offline tasks take precedence, screen time is controlled, and activities like cooking, exercising, and reading are given importance. It's a lifestyle that encourages mindful living, helping me appreciate the simple joys of life. While it might not be everyone's cup of tea, it has proven to be a fulfilling and sustainable approach for me in navigating the demands of the digital age.

Chapter 10

Creating a Low Tech Lifestyle

Creating a low tech lifestyle may seem like a daunting task in our increasingly connected and digital world. However, it can be a powerful way to reduce stress, increase focus, and improve overall well-being. By limiting screen time, prioritizing offline activities, and finding new ways to connect with the world around us, we can create a more intentional and fulfilling life. In this guide, we will explore practical tips and strategies for creating a low tech lifestyle, from purging excess digital clutter to embracing new hobbies and activities that keep us engaged and present in the moment.

Step 1: Make an Inventory and Categorize

Just as we undertake the ritual of spring or fall cleaning, decluttering our physical spaces, it's equally important to cleanse our digital landscape. The first step in this journey involves taking stock of our digital possessions - the array of apps and services spread across our desktop and mobile devices. This process is not merely about listing what we have, but understanding how, when, and why we use these digital tools. Fortunately, modern smartphones are equipped with built-in utilities that can shed light on our digital behavior. Android phones offer 'Digital Wellbeing' under settings, and iOS devices provide 'Screen Time' as a resource. These applications not only identify what apps we frequent but also track their usage duration and the times at which we access them. For a comprehensive view of our digital interactions, we can rely on desktop tools like Clockify or Rescue Time for our PCs, regardless of whether we use a Mac or Windows. These tools, many of which are free, provide an insightful overview of the services, apps, and software we interact with on our computers.

Reflecting on a personal experience, I recall the transformative process of downsizing from a spacious four-bedroom home in Georgia to a compact two-bedroom condo in Littleton, CO. The move necessitated a careful assessment of our belongings, a journey of deciding what was essential and what could be relinquished. Initial reluctance gave way to an almost therapeutic process of letting go of unnecessary items. We donated, sold, and discarded various belongings that were either unused or had outlived their usefulness. It was a cathartic experience, unburdening us from the weight of the unnecessary and enabling us to embrace our new home with only those possessions that truly mattered. This poignant experience underscored the importance of regular evaluation of our possessions and conscious decision-making about what we retain.

In the digital realm, the process of assessment and categorization requires the same level of intentionality and thoughtfulness. Begin by identifying the digital tools that are indispensable to your daily life - those that facilitate vital communication and work-related tasks. These could include your phone, messaging apps, or encrypted communication platforms like Signal. Following that, ponder over the apps that enrich your day, adding value without monopolizing your time or attention. Podcasts, music players, and navigation apps could fall into this category. It's equally crucial to recognize the apps that serve as distractions, those that incessantly clamor for your attention and hamper productivity. Social media platforms, email apps, and news services, especially those that can be accessed via desktop, often fall into this category. Lastly, consider the apps that are essential for professional or academic activities, such as email, Slack, Notion, or calendar apps. By systematically categorizing your digital tools, you can streamline your digital interactions, relegating nonessential apps to the periphery and bringing the essential ones to the forefront. This will pave the way for a more conscious, intentional, and ultimately fulfilling low-tech lifestyle, mirroring the liberation and tranquility that come with decluttering physical spaces. To make it clearer, here is my list of apps and services:

- **Essential**: These are the tools that I rely on daily, facilitating vital communication and work-related tasks. They form the backbone of my professional and personal interactions.

    - **Light Phone 2:** It's a tool for communication, entertainment, and nothing addictive.

    - **Email:** I use a standalone application (Thunderbird or Outlook) and restrict it to my laptop or desktop.

    - **Colibri:** This is a browser that can only open one tab at a time. I open my work management website with it and get my work done. Also, on my laptop/desktop.

- **Nice to Have Apps**: These are the apps that enrich my day and add value without monopolizing my time or attention. They generally enhance my well-being or simplify my life.

    - **Navigation Apps**: A garmin GPS in the car provides reliable directions when on the move.

    - **Podcasts**: I use the Light Phone 2's basic podcast tool to listen to insightful conversations and learn new things.

- **Music Players**: I own an mp3 player for loading my favorite playlists.

* **Potential Distractions**: These are the apps and platforms that can be a source of distraction, interrupting my focus, and eating into my productive time.

  - **Social Media Platforms**: Facebook, Instagram, and Twitter can be major distractions. I use these only for business purposes and do not have access to them except at the office for work.

  - **News Apps**: While these are important, they can be distracting when accessed too frequently. I use Readwise to clip articles that I may find useful. Later in the day, I read 3 stories and eliminate stories that are not helpful.

* **Professional and Academic Necessities**: These are tools that are necessary for my job and academic pursuits.

  - **Teams**: This is a key tool for team communication in my work environment. I use it on desktop and laptop.

- **Notion**: I use Notion as a comprehensive workspace to write, plan, and get organized.

- **Calendar Apps**: Google Calendar helps me keep track of all my appointments and deadlines online. I only put it there after I have locked down my week on a paper calendar.

Step 2: Quit Services

Embarking on the journey towards a low-tech lifestyle requires careful evaluation of our digital dependencies. The process might be time-consuming and the longest step in this endeavor, but undoubtedly, it is the most pivotal one. Identifying the essential applications and services in our lives is the first milestone. What follows next is the challenging task of discerning the value and impact of the remaining apps, and deciding whether they need to be excised from our digital routine. It's important to remember that while some apps may appear to enrich our lives, they often serve as disguised distractions, detracting from our productivity and impinging on our overall well-being.

Consider popular social media platforms, such as Facebook, Instagram, and Twitter, for instance. They can indeed create a sense of connectedness and offer a platform for self-expression. However, they can also be insidiously addictive, subtly demanding your attention through constant notifications, luring you into the vortex of infinite scrolling. If you notice that significant chunks of your day are consumed by these platforms, it might be an indication to delete these apps and regain control over your digital footprint. Streaming services like Netflix and Hulu can also become inadvertent culprits of our digital fatigue. While they serve as a source of entertainment, the compulsive consumption of content, or binge-watching, can monopolize your time. If this pattern sounds familiar, it may be beneficial to reassess your subscriptions, possibly even canceling them. Redirecting this time towards screen-free hobbies like reading, painting, hiking, or any other activity that ignites your passion can be an excellent alternative.

Equally crucial is to contemplate the psychological implications of your digital consumption. Are there specific apps that consistently trigger stress, anxiety, or feelings of inadequacy? It's essential to reassess their role in your life. The action could range from limiting their usage to certain periods or removing them from your devices entirely. The guiding principle of a low-tech lifestyle is to prioritize your mental well-being and happiness, so any app that undermines this should be critically evaluated. Furthermore, it's essential to establish clear boundaries if your work requires you to use social media or messaging apps. Deleting personal profiles and creating separate professional accounts can help preserve a healthy work-life balance. It can also assist in resisting the temptation to check work-related notifications outside of designated working hours.

The essence of the second step is about asserting control over our digital world. It's about choosing judiciously which services are worth retaining and which ones need to be discarded. The guiding principle is quite straightforward: if an application or service consumes more time than it contributes to productivity, it might be time to let it go. However, if a tool is indispensable for professional purposes, consider segregating it through a dedicated app or device, thus minimizing the potential for distraction. And as for those apps that do bring value but are potentially time-consuming, it's crucial to devise strategies to manage their use effectively. This leads us to our next step: the implementation of 'time zones'. Time zones are specific periods during your day dedicated to certain tasks or activities, including the use of particular apps or services. This approach ensures you're enjoying these value-added services without them encroaching on your productivity or relaxation time. The commitment to this process, to carefully evaluate and reduce unnecessary digital interactions, forms the bedrock of this transformative journey. It necessitates patience, resilience, and conscious effort, but the rewards it offers are substantial. The possibility of a more intentional and fulfilling life, where technology serves us rather than dictates us, is indeed a pursuit that's worth every bit of the effort.

Step 3: Time Zones

In the digital era, time is indeed our most valuable asset. Despite being a seasoned digital minimalist, I've experienced periods of exceptional productivity interspersed with times of excessive screen attraction. Regardless of your current stage, remember that change is possible with purpose and determination. That's precisely where step 3—implementing "time zones"—plays a pivotal role. "Time zones" in the context of digital minimalism are a structured approach to managing time, allowing us to be more purposeful with our digital and non-digital interactions. They come in two forms: Offline and Online Zones. Offline zones are dedicated periods where all online activities are put on hold. This means no devices, no digital disruptions—nothing that might reconnect you to the online world. Offline zones are reserved for activities that do not require a digital medium—think engaging conversations, hands-on hobbies like woodworking, meditative walks in the park, or simply the act of being present in your surroundings.

Online zones, conversely, are windows of time specifically set aside for online activities. This could include listening to podcasts, checking social media, responding to emails, or any task requiring your digital presence. However, the aim is to choose activities that belong to the 'essential', 'nice to have', and 'operations' categories, identified in Step 1. Time-wasting activities should ideally be minimized or eliminated altogether during these periods. For maximum efficiency, consider using a paper or digital calendar to map out your time zones. Allocate blocks of time for various activities, and color-code them for visual appeal and better organization. For instance, you might color offline zones in calming blue and online zones in invigorating red. This not only stimulates your brain aesthetically but also enhances organization and clarity.

By structuring your day around these time zones, you regain control over your digital interactions, enhancing productivity and reducing digital clutter. For instance, if you're a writer, you could schedule your offline zone in the morning for drafting and brainstorming, followed by an online zone in the afternoon for research and correspondence. This approach allows you to focus on one type of task at a time, reducing the cognitive load of constant digital shifting. Moreover, time zones can be tailored to your specific lifestyle and profession. A software developer might need longer online zones for coding and debugging, while a yoga instructor might require longer offline zones for classes and personal practice.

Ultimately, the implementation of time zones is not about adhering to a rigid schedule but about gaining a deeper awareness of our digital habits and making intentional changes that align with our values and goals. It is about reclaiming our time from the clutches of digital excess and channeling it towards more fulfilling, meaningful endeavors. Remember, it's not about perfection, but progression. Your initial attempt at defining time zones may not work perfectly, and that's okay. Adjust, learn, and refine as you go along. The journey to digital minimalism is a marathon, not a sprint, and every small step you take brings you closer to a more intentional and fulfilling digital life.

Step 4: Companions (another name for accountability and helpful tools)

Embarking on the journey toward digital minimalism can be an arduous endeavor, and one that is not advisable to pursue in isolation. This path is strewn with obstacles that necessitate not only an unwavering personal commitment but also the support of a community and the shared responsibility that comes with it. This introduces us to Step 4: Companions. This stage emphasizes the critical need to establish a network of individuals who share similar goals and to leverage tools and resources that can assist us in navigating this journey. Acknowledging our susceptibility to digital temptations and accepting the fact that we might need help are key elements of this transformative journey.

Our smartphones have evolved into a virtual multipurpose tool, offering a broad spectrum of capabilities. This, however, is a double-edged sword. While the convenience of having a single device that can execute a multitude of tasks is undeniable, this very adaptability can serve as a snare, drawing us into an abyss of perpetual distractions. The technology industry, with its persuasive narratives and polished marketing strategies, has coaxed us into subscribing to the belief that this amalgamation of functionalities into a solitary device is advantageous. It is high time we challenge this conception. Reclaiming our autonomy over our digital lives necessitates a reevaluation and diversification of our gadget portfolio. This does not imply an impulsive spree to acquire the latest devices; rather, it entails a conscious selection of tools that resonate with our needs and foster our progression toward digital minimalism. This could involve investing in distinct devices for various tasks such as listening to music, navigating, reading, and watching shows. This approach might seem counterintuitive and potentially expensive, but it's a long-term investment toward diminishing our dependence on the omnifarious smartphone and reestablishing control over our digital consumption.

For instance, one could consider investing in a standalone music player like an iPod or a high-resolution digital audio player. A device like the Sony Walkman NW-A105, which allows the option to download and play music offline, can reduce the reliance on your smartphone for music, thereby limiting potential distractions. These specialized devices offer superior sound quality and battery life compared to smartphones, promising an immersive, uninterrupted musical journey. This shift is about reclaiming the delight of listening to music without the incessant interruptions of notifications, calls, or the lurking temptation to check social media. Choosing such dedicated devices over the multipurpose smartphone might seem like a technological regression. However, in terms of personal well-being and productivity, it's a significant stride forward. It is a deliberate decision to prioritize the quality of experience over convenience, to treasure presence over pervasive connectivity. Investing in separate devices can also help streamline your digital experience. For example, a Kindle e-reader can greatly enhance your reading experience. Unlike smartphones or tablets, e-readers are designed solely for reading, offering a distraction-free environment that closely mimics the experience of reading a physical book. The e-ink technology reduces eye strain, and the long-lasting battery life ensures you can immerse yourself in a book without worrying about charging the device. This might seem like an extra expense, but consider it an investment in your well-being. These devices allow you to enjoy the benefits of digital technology without the constant barrage of notifications and distractions inherent in multipurpose devices like smartphones.

Another vital aspect of this journey is acknowledging when we require external support. Internet and Technology Addicts Anonymous (ITAA) is an invaluable resource for individuals wrestling with the allure of the digital world. They extend guidance, foster a supportive community, and proffer practical strategies to manage and eventually overcome internet and technology addiction. Their sponsorship program and frequent meetings provide the necessary encouragement and motivation, reinforcing the fact that we are not alone in this struggle. Embracing this challenge calls for bravery, humility, and often, a shift in perspective. Digital minimalism is not merely a lifestyle choice, but a declaration of our personal agency in a world increasingly dominated by digital consumption. It is a quest to rediscover the profundity of human experience that extends beyond the boundaries of screens, to recognize the worth of our attention, and to invest it in pursuits that genuinely enrich our lives. This journey may be laden with setbacks and trials, but the rewards – in terms of enhanced control over our time, improved mental health, and a more meaningful life – are immense. And remember, you don't have to traverse this path alone. Seeking help, whether from organizations like ITAA or from a supportive community of like-minded individuals, is an expression of strength, not a sign of weakness.

As you embark on this journey of digital minimalism, remember that it's okay to feel uncertain or overwhelmed at times. The goal is not to achieve perfection but to make consistent, mindful choices that align with your values and aspirations. Each step taken towards reducing digital clutter is a step towards a more balanced and fulfilling life.

Step 5: Repeat

The journey to digital minimalism is not a one-time sprint but a continuous marathon. It requires ongoing commitment, evaluation, and recalibration, thus leading us to the fifth step: Repeat. This step is the crux of the process, emphasizing the importance of continual reassessment and adjustment. It's about understanding that this journey isn't a linear one and that you'll need to periodically reevaluate your relationship with technology and make necessary adjustments.

To embark on this process, it's beneficial to take a step back every quarter or biannually to reassess your digital consumption habits and evaluate your progress towards your goals. This doesn't just mean tracking how much time you're spending on different platforms or apps, but also asking yourself deeper, introspective questions. Are your current digital habits serving your larger life goals and values? Are they enhancing your well-being or causing stress and distraction? How can you refine your strategies to better align with your aspirations for a more balanced, intentional digital life?

A fundamental part of this process is visualizing the lifestyle you desire and working backwards from that vision to set achievable goals. This could mean envisioning a day where you can read a book without checking your phone every few minutes, or a workday where you can focus on tasks without being interrupted by incessant notifications. What does a balanced, fulfilling digital life look like for you? Once you have a clear picture of what you want to achieve, you can then start crafting strategies and making changes to move closer to that vision.

Remember, digital minimalism isn't about completely eliminating digital technology from your life, but about using it in a way that serves you, not the other way around. It's about reclaiming your time and attention from the relentless demands of the digital world and investing them in activities and relationships that truly matter to you. In essence, the repeat step is your commitment to a cycle of continuous learning and improvement. It's your promise to yourself that you will regularly reassess, readjust, and refine your digital habits to better serve your vision of a fulfilling, intentional life. This process may be challenging, but the rewards—a sense of control over your digital life, greater focus and productivity, and a more balanced and fulfilling lifestyle—make it a pursuit worth undertaking.

Chapter 11

Conclusion

The California sun was warm on my face as I sat across from my grandmother, my Abuelita, her lined face a testament to a life lived fully. A pang of guilt resonated within me, a haunting echo of missed opportunities from past visits. The ghostly memories of unseized moments hung in the air between us. But, there was a different resolve in me this time. This visit, I was committed to not just being there, but truly being present. The familiar hum of the television buzzed in the backdrop, its flickering screen vying for attention. Yet, I made a choice. I chose to focus on the woman in front of me, to indulge in her experiences, to savor the timbre of her voice as she recounted tales of her recent trip back to our hometown. There was a rich tapestry of family lore and bygone eras in her words, in her laughter. Our conversation, though not lengthy, was teeming with the authenticity of connection.

Our interaction was interrupted by my dog, a ball of impatience curling at our feet, his eager eyes pleading for

CONCLUSION 165

his walk. As Abuelita and I navigated through the verdant landscapes of the nearby park, our conversation flowed like a gentle stream, punctuated with shared laughter and fond remembrances. It was a simple, unassuming moment, its ordinary nature belying the profundity it held. These strolls, these shared stories reminded me that the euphoria of the digital world, that instant dopamine rush, is not the sole path to joy. The essence of life, I realized, was often found in the smallest moments, those unscripted instants of connection that root us to our world and our loved ones. The real value lay not in digital engagement, but in human engagement, in the power of presence.

This experience, this beautiful encapsulation of slow living, punctuated my thoughts as I penned this book. I realized that the essence of a low-tech life wasn't solely about reducing our screen time, but more about enhancing our life time – about accentuating human connections and enriching experiences. Through this book, my aim has been to kindle in you a desire to live mindfully, to value the simple, often overlooked moments that life generously offers. To encourage you to decelerate in this fast-paced world, to truly connect with the world and the people around you. To find delight in the ordinary and tranquility in the routine. Because, when all is said and done, it's people and moments that enrich our lives the most.

Epilogue

The journey you and I have embarked on through the pages of this book has not been merely about managing our devices or tweaking our digital habits. It's been a much grander exploration, an introspective expedition into understanding our values, our connections, and the inherent human need for presence and meaningful experiences. It has been about questioning the fast-paced, always-on digital culture we find ourselves in, and daring to choose a different path.

In every chapter, I've shared stories, insights, and practical steps to guide you towards a Low Tech Life. These stories are not just tales of personal transformation, but reminders of what truly matters in life. They serve as tokens of a world that values deep human connections over digital interactions, present moments over past regrets or future anxieties, and simplicity over complexity.

We've embraced the idea that technology is a tool, not a master. We've learned to set boundaries, explored the necessity of companions in our journey, and recognized the importance of reassessment and iteration. We have learned that living a Low Tech Life is not about completely shunning technology, but about creating a harmonious relationship with it.

It's not a one-size-fits-all process, but rather, a deeply personal journey that requires patience and commitment. I have no doubt that you will encounter challenges along the way. There may be moments of discomfort, even frustration. But remember, these are not signs of failure, but of growth.

One of the most important things I hope you take away from this book is that you are not alone in this journey. There's a growing community of digital minimalists around the world who, like you, are striving for a more balanced, meaningful life. Reach out, engage, and learn from them. Together, we can create a culture that values human connection over digital consumption.

As I close the final pages of this book, my heart is filled with gratitude. I am profoundly thankful that you have joined me on this journey. I hope that the stories, insights, and strategies shared here inspire you to embrace the Low Tech Life, not as a rigid set of rules, but as a fluid philosophy that evolves with you.

And as you move forward in this journey, remember to take a moment to appreciate the simple joys of life - the warmth of the sun on your face, the laughter of a loved one, the beauty of a quiet morning. Because at the end of the day, it is these moments, the ones we often overlook in our hurried, screen-saturated lives, that truly matter.

Here's to living a Low Tech Life, one that honors our humanity amidst the hum of the digital world. Thank you for embarking on this journey with me. Remember, it's not the destination, but the journey that truly matters. And this journey is just beginning...

Printed in Great Britain
by Amazon